The Archers
The Ambridge CHRONICLES

The Archers
The Ambridge CHRONICLES

MOMENTS THAT MADE THE NATION'S FAVOURITE RADIO DRAMA

JOANNA TOYE
AND KAREN FARRINGTON

This book is published to accompany the BBC Radio 4 series *The Archers*

Vanessa Whitburn edited *The Archers* from 1992 to 2013.

3 5 7 9 10 8 6 4 2

Published in 2013 by BBC Books, an imprint of Ebury Publishing.
A Random House Group Company.

Script extracts written by: Debbie Cook, Mary Cutler, Paul Burns, Tessa Diamond, John Fletcher, Adrian Flynn, Simon Frith, Nawal Gadalla, Caroline Harrington, Graham Harvey, Christopher Hawes, Brian Hayles, Sam Jacobs, Peter Kerry, Helen Leadbeater, Malcolm Lynch, Edward J Mason, Bruno Milna, James Robson, Carole Simpson Solazzo, Tim Stimpson, Chris Thompson, Joanna Toye and Geoffrey Webb.

While every effort has been made to trace and acknowledge script writers, we would like to apologise should there be any errors or omissions.

The Random House Group Limited Reg. No. 954009

Addresses for companies within the Random House Group can be found at www.randomhouse.co.uk

A CIP catalogue record for this book is available from the British Library.

ISBN: 9781849905770

The Random House Group Limited supports the Forest Stewardship Council® (FSC®), the leading international forest-certification organisation. Our books carrying the FSC label are printed on FSC®-certified paper. FSC is the only forest-certification scheme supported by the leading environmental organisations, including Greenpeace. Our paper procurement policy can be found at www.randomhouse.co.uk/environment

Commissioning editor: Albert DePetrillo
Project editors: Nicholas Payne, Laura Higginson and Lizzy Gaisford
Designer: O'Leary & Cooper
Production: Phil Spencer

Printed and bound by CPI Group (UK) Ltd, Croydon, CR0 4YY

CONTENTS

INTRODUCTION

'The problem has always been not to find but to choose,' wrote Dr Watson about his seventeen years' worth of notes on Sherlock Holmes's twenty-three years of detecting. Lucky Watson! With almost sixty-three years of *The Archers* on air and over 17,000 scripts – stored on disc, tape and CD, on paper and microfilm, card index and computer – our problem was both in the choosing and the finding.

There were helpful suggestions from listeners, cast, writers and production team; there were also folk memories, which were the most difficult and sometimes impossible to track down: 'A lovely episode where Phil and Tom went fishing…' didn't narrow it down much. While the saga of Ned Larkin's first encounter with a zipped fly on his trousers – pretty revolutionary in 1950s Ambridge, it seems, at least for a farmworker – led to apparently hilarious consequences which sadly remain frustratingly elusive. However, there were plenty of other incidents to choose from…

The most exciting challenge was selecting the actual script extracts. Previous books have retold storylines and quoted snippets of script, but we wanted to present entire sections of dialogue – sometimes almost entire scenes – to help tell the story but also to recreate the mood of a particular moment. Would they work on the page or did you need to 'be there', in the sense of hearing them played out? Would scripts from the 1950s come over with their full period charm? It soon became clear that the words had a resonance of their own, and the book also uses a lot of script material that has never before been reproduced, giving a new dimension to emblematic *Archers* events – the death of Grace, for example, or the Grundys' eviction from Grange Farm.

Many people deserve special thanks. *Archers* Editor Vanessa Whitburn has been a staunch support throughout, and the fount of all knowledge, *Archers* Archivist Camilla Fisher, stimulated ideas as well as helped to source specific scripts. At BBC Books, Nicholas Payne and Laura Higginson provided editorial support, while Jeff Walden at BBC Written Archives was a great help in digging out older material. Writers past and present generously gave permission for their dialogue to be reproduced – not forgetting the skill over the years of various production teams and technical crews, and the magnificent *Archers* cast, which made it so memorable in the first place.

With so much material, the result is inevitably partial, personal and totally idiosyncratic – but whether the book surprises with the unknown, revives memories or even provokes cries of 'Oh, but what about…?' then its job is done. Heartbreak and happiness, triumph and tragedy, wit and wisdom – they're all here for you to enjoy.

Joanna Toye and Karen Farrington

COUNTRY LIFE

FARMERS HAVE ALWAYS BEEN key to the nation's prosperity and wellbeing and Dan Archer was among an army of farmers getting Britain back on its feet following the Second World War. Indeed, farmers were domestic heroes as they laboured to restore the country's larders after long-term privation.

Mechanisation was all a-go-go and the future looked bright, with the Archers benefitting from subsidies paid for the production of cereal crops to combat a continuing shortfall in food supply. Some things subsequently changed, like the way farms were staffed and crops were harvested. In 1973, after Britain joined the Common Market, as it was then called, there were still more transformations. Although a later referendum returned a resounding 'yes' to membership from the British, Phil Archer was concerned that no one could predict the future. He told father Dan: 'If you mix various colours together you get a different colour; and then if you add one more colour you might either get the prettiest effect you ever saw or a muddy-looking mess…'

Some things stayed the same and the joys of country living were still keenly understood among those who largely felt privileged to grow up among pasture and pigs instead of traffic and tower blocks.

Alas, farms were still subject to the ravages of dreadful diseases, with all the associated heartache. To combat the challenges in farming, Pat and Tony were early converts to the organic movement while Brian Aldridge put his faith in high-spec modern methods. Some failed to respond and didn't survive. The Grundys were among the victims of changing times, when cold, economic reality pushes people to the depths of despair.

TRACTOR FACTOR

According to Tom Forrest, the first tractor to chug its way through Ambridge was an International Harvester that belonged to Squire Lawson-Hope. However, Joe believed the ubiquitous Standard Fordson owned by George Fairbrother as early as 1934 was the district's first mechanised farm machinery. Thanks to Dan Archer's diary, there's no doubt that his first tractor was an old, grey Ferguson bought in 1951 and used in place of two beloved Shire horses. Indeed, it wasn't until after the Second World War with a major drive for food production inspired by government policies that tractors became a common sight in the British countryside. Britain became known as 'the stockyard of the world' – and Ambridge certainly played its part.

THE WAY WE WERE

As time marches by, incremental adjustments to daily life follow in its wake. Ultimately these add up to some substantial step changes that have shaped the lives of those in Ambridge and beyond. Things that were once routine have been reduced to a memory that's dusted down on high days and holidays. Reminiscences like these give insight into the way we were, warming the soul as much as any roaring log fire ever could.

Joe Grundy remembers the 'penny auctions' in the 1930s when small farmers 'used to stand together against the big boys'. There was a particular one at Turner's Farm, which he recalls with a fond chuckle:

> My dad took me up there. The Turners were being turned out by the bank so the bank were auctioning off all their belongings, trying to wring the last drop out of them. So all the small farmers met up beforehand and decided on what they were going to do. Come the auction, the plough goes up, only one bloke bids for it – one penny. Then the binder… one penny. Went all through the machinery, then the livestock… in the end, the bank had fifteen shillings to put in their vault.

Manpower on farms has dwindled while machines have proliferated and Jill for one has noticed the way the feel of farming has changed because of it:

> That's the trouble with farming these days. There are so few people to draw on at busy times. When I think what it was like in our day. You had all the staff and their families and for the big things, like lambing and haymaking, everyone seemed willing to help.

In November 1973, Tony's then fiancée Mary Weston went away on a Farm Secretary's Course – 'learning about metrication among other things'.

Today plastic bags are seen as the scourge of society, with no self-respecting shopper leaving a supermarket with one in hand. Back in the days when Martha Woodford ran the shop, it was a different story, with Vicar Richard Adamson expressing particular delight in them.

VICAR	Handy, these polythene bags.
MARTHA	Yes, lots of shops are giving them away these days. Ones this size are real useful.
VICAR	If you don't mind advertising somebody's supermarket.
MARTHA	(LAUGHING) I don't mind who you advertise as long as you do your shopping here.

In 1957, at a time of full employment – and when the idea of East European workers from beyond 'the Iron Curtain' in the countryside would have been not just laughed at but feared – Dan was worried about staffing on the farm. The potatoes needed lifting, so he planned to 'pop into Borchester Labour Exchange to see if they've got anybody on their books who'll come and do the job'.

When it came to a full-time worker, however, life was more problematical. 'The only way I'd get a chap is pinch him from somebody else and pay him over the odds to stay with me,' he fretted to Doris. There was, however, hope on the horizon: 'The secretary of the NFU can put me on to the district apprenticeship committee and I can make an application to them… then one or two members of the committee'll come out here and inspect us… to see whether we're suitable people to have an apprentice and if the sort of farming I do is likely to give the lad a good training.'

'Well!' exclaimed Doris in outrage. 'Particular, aren't they?'

In 1981, Phil faced the same problem when David planned a gap year on a farm in Holland to gain wider experience. But at the time the 1980s were yet to boom, in the Midlands at least, and so the British government was being proactive, as he told Jill:

> I had a letter from the careers people this morning. They're trying to find jobs for young people in the area and want to know if I can offer anything… these kids are wanting to do an apprenticeship or a year before they go to college… I don't necessarily have to take someone permanently. Just to fill David's place really.

The 1980s were the last gasp of the post-war farming boom. There have been good years since for various branches of farming ('Up corn, down horn' and vice versa, as the old country saying goes), but in general, owing to mechanisation – and cost-cutting – it's been a case of shedding staff and employing more family labour, casuals and ex-farm staff who've turned self-employed.

Neil Carter used to work full time as Brookfield's pigman; Mike Tucker was a tenant farmer, as was Eddie Grundy. Both Mike and Eddie lost their farms and now do various sorts of freelance work, though happily Ed Grundy has been reinstalled at Grange Farm.

After Brian Aldridge came to Ambridge in 1975 and began dating Jennifer, he confessed, 'I'm a fool for a gadget.' The gadget in question? A pocket calculator. Eleven years later, the calculator had still failed to win Martha Woodford's trust, though. She refused to use one in the village shop, resulting in sometimes lengthy queues as she added up with paper and pen.

On 11 March 1952, the Archer clan gathered around the radio to hear Conservative chancellor Rab Butler's budget. 'I propose that the single allowance shall be increased from £110 to £120, the married allowance from £190 to £210 and the child allowance from £70 to £85,' he declared.

The financial plans got a guarded thumbs up around the farm table, with Dan Archer hoping that people in Britain would one day understand how much it cost to grow food. Sixty years later, the personal tax allowance stood at £7,475, with married allowances largely obsolete, being available only to those who wed before 1935.

For the record, the close of Butler's speech – not aired on radio via *The Archers* – had remarkably similar themes to those we hear from politicians today…

> But what is more, all its changes – the new revenue, and the savings from further economies – are being devoted to relieving hardship, reducing inequity and providing fresh incentives. Solvency, security, duty and incentive are our themes. Restriction and austerity are not enough. We want a system which offers us both more realism and more hope.

It's frustrating enough for Ambridge farmers – and their friends and families – when they're out of range or leave their mobiles behind but communications were far more difficult in the past. Calls to and from Ambridge went through the local 'exchange' and the rarity of the telephone was reflected in the numbers allocated: the phone number of the village shop in 1951 was Ambridge 14.

When Phil met Jill in the mid-1950s, she was a demonstrator of kitchen equipment, and he had to write to her at her lodgings as she travelled all over the country, or rely on her landladies to pass on phone – or rather 'telephone' – messages. Waiting for Jill to return a call, he was so anxious that he arrived a whole hour late for supper at Brookfield, asking if they'd had a call for him and explaining: 'Before I came out I rang the Trunks people and said if a number should come through from Birmingham for Combe Farm this evening to transfer it here.'

'From Birmingham?' queried an incredulous Doris, as if he'd said Bogota.

She was at this point still unaware of the liaison. Trunk calls were calls from beyond the local exchange.

As late as 1973, the big news which greeted Mrs P on return from a trip away was that her daughter Peggy had had a phone installed in her mother's bungalow, though at least Peggy had had proper engineers in, unlike Walter's attempt at a DIY television set on which he and Mrs P could watch the Coronation in 1953.

Things weren't much easier in the 1980s when the best and sometimes only way to contact someone travelling on the Continent – or even sometimes in the British Isles – in a life-threatening emergency was to put out a message on Radio 4. The Archer family almost qualified for one when a battery blew up in Phil's face, causing an eye injury. With David dawdling back through France from a year-long placement in Holland ('We tried to contact you, believe me. Left little messages in cleft sticks all round Europe…'), Shula was left to run things with farm workers Neil Carter and Jethro Larkin.

When David did reappear, Jethro, never in the vanguard of the Women's Liberation movement, was relieved, as he confided in his new son-in-law, Eddie:

JETHRO	Makes no end of difference, having a proper bloke in charge again.
EDDIE	Don't see why.
JETHRO	You wouldn't. Probably never seen one in action. I told Miss Shula that field of barley wanted doing urgent. She means well, but she don't know how to get things moving.
EDDIE	You gonna tell her that to her face?
JETHRO	No point in hurting the girl's feelings. But young Master David, now. Comes home last night, takes one look at the place and sees what's what.

First light, he's out there with the combine, no mucking about.

EDDIE On his own? Who's driving the trailer?

JETHRO Well, Shula's helping him, of course. Only natural she would, isn't it?

But technology was moving on in Ambridge, inexorably. Nigel had an Instamatic camera in 1984 and John a computer (for his pig accounts) in 1990, by which time Joe's cash card had long been swallowed by the 'hole in the wall'. Brian had a mobile phone as early as 1992 and, though it was 'a bit dicky', Ruth was keen that Brookfield should get one. In the same year she asked Nigel's advice about a fax machine for the farm office. Nowadays, the village has its own website and Pip has a Smartphone with lots of apps; while Tom's sausages and ready meals have their own Facebook pages and Twitter followers. Several of the village children are welded to their computer games and Skype calls are a regular feature of farming and family life.

TASTE TEST

Almost all milk is now heat-treated or pasteurised, but older Ambridge characters still eulogise about the taste of milk in the days when the farmer's wife used to go and dip a jug in the bulk tank for the family's supplies.

As Mary Pound recalled: 'In good milk you should be able to taste the grass. I could always tell when the cows had been grazing Dyson's Field because of all the wild thyme in the grass – you could taste it. Good milk's alive. That in bottles tastes dead – like ashes,' she concluded.

COUNTRY LORE

'Wineberry, wigtail, tarradiddle, den…' Phil Archer was puzzled when he heard his farmworker Jethro muttering this strange incantation in a Brookfield sheep-pasture. 'Onetherum, twotherum, cockerum, catherum, shetherum, shatherum….'

Not sure whether to blame a touch of the sun, he was mightily relieved when Jethro enlightened him: it was an old system of sheep-counting. 'Each word counts two sheep,' Jethro explained, 'and when you've said all the words, that's twenty, so you hold up one finger. Means you can count up to a hundred on one hand.'

After Phil and David marvelled, college-educated David even going so far as to eulogise the amount of traditional know-how that's passed on from generation to generation, Jethro revealed the truth.

He hadn't learnt the system from his dad; he'd cribbed it out of a book on folklore his daughter Clarrie had got out of the library – in a poignant (and unsuccessful) attempt to concoct a potion to make Eddie Grundy propose to her.

PLUS ÇA CHANGE...

If every conversation about weather, the cost of living and the shortcomings of the incumbent government have a familiar ring, well, it's because it's pretty much all been said before. The concerns aired around the kitchen table fifty years ago have sufficient currency today to carry them through for a few more decades yet. As it's often been observed, the more things change, the more they stay the same.

We think of global warming as a recent concern, but it's been observed in Ambridge for years. Way back in the mid-1970s, gamekeeper Tom Forrest was keeping a weather eye on things.

TOM	Harrowing already, I see. Earlier than last year in't you?
JETHRO	I suppose we are a bit. Put it down to the weather.

TOM You can put a lot down to this weather – never knows where we are with it. Remember January? Daffodils in flower?

JETHRO Ah, maybe them scientists is right. Maybe the seasons are changing.

TOM Well summat's gone cock-eyed that's for certain. I can remember blazing hot summers and winters with snow up to here – all that seems to have gone.

JETHRO 'Cording to what I seen on the telly things is evening out – leastways some parts of the world they are.

TOM I suppose we shouldn't grumble but it makes a nonsense of what us gets to learn by experience, doesn't it?

JETHRO Some things still holds good – some of the sayings like red sky in the morning, shepherds' warning.

TOM Ah mebbe. But I was thinking about more practical things. Like when we was having our shoots back at Christmas. When it gets cold, the pheasants all gets together in the woods or the spinneys but it's been so blessed mild, they don't find the need for it. It's been harder work putting up the birds because of that.

The terminology's changed but farmers – and others – still complain bitterly about the amount of red tape and form-filling that EU bureaucracy requires, as Dan did to his son-in-law Paul Johnson in 1976 when Paul tried to talk to him about his horsebox business: 'Sorry, Paul. Coping with Price Reviews and Common Market jargon is enough for me, thanks.'

When Jethro gave a report to regulars at The Bull about his May bank holiday outing in 1973, it had a fearfully familiar ring:

JETHRO	I was just telling Sid about me getting caught in that traffic jam on the way to Netherbourne.
DAN	You didn't go that way, did you?
JETHRO	I did! Lizzie and the two girls and me mother. And by the time we'd got filled up wi' petrol and been round to pick me mother up, I thought we might as well go Netherbourne way, see?

DAN Rather you than me. They've got the road up.

JETHRO I know that now. And there was a multiple accident. So us 'ad three hours in the car... Lizzie got one of her heads, and as soon as the traffic started moving we just went up to the Netherbourne roundabout, round it and straight back 'ome.

DAN Hardly an afternoon out!

JETHRO I've said it afore, I'll say it again. Never no more.

A HARD LESSON

When Shula Archer wanted to find herself in the 1970s, she went off to Bangkok; when Kate Aldridge wanted to do the same in the 1990s, she went off to Morocco. In the 1950s, things were simpler, and when four students rented Pru Harris's cottage in Ambridge in the summer of 1957, expressing a desire to get close to country life, there was no shortage of manual labouring jobs to bring them very close indeed. For one of them in particular, a boy named Crofton, it was a baptism of fire…

His first task was stooking corn. Luckily he could learn from the best:

DAN (RUSTLE OF SHEAVES) Bang 'em down well, now, won't you, 'cos if you don't they're liable to collapse.

CROFTON Yes... (GRUNT OF EFFORT) This job's all right for the first hour or two. Expect it can get tiring when you have to do it all day, though, can't it?

DAN Certainly can... So can pitching the sheaves up onto the cart or stack, my lad. That'll find your weak muscles quicker than anything...

CROFTON I can imagine...

DAN You can bang 'em down harder than that.

CROFTON Sorry.

DAN That's the idea, boy. You're getting it fine. Best not to trust to the knots in the binder twine too much, though...

There was even time for a bottle of cold tea ('Missus sent it down for you. Nothing like it as a refresher') and, to Dan's amusement, a quick nature lesson about a brood of partridge (Crofton's wild guess was that the birds were moorhens). Then, after a day in the broiling sun, the poor boy moved on to his next task, cutting back the hedges and brambles round the cottage where the lads were staying. But Tom Forrest, then courting Pru, and out for an evening stroll with her, soon scented trouble:

	(FADE IN SOUND OF BRAMBLES CRACKLING AND BLAZING IN BACKGROUND)
TOM	(SNIFFING) Hullo. Someone's got a fire burning.
PRU	It must be Crofton clearing and burning the brambles from my place.
TOM	Well, if he gets that too high he's asking for trouble... (SWELL CRACKLE) There's a field of standing corn next to us and the wind's taking it right over! It's as dry as tinder! A couple of sparks in that lot and the whole blessed field'll go up...

Tom and Pru raced to the scene and, with Tom berating him, poor Crofton inadvertently made things worse:

TOM	No, no, no! Don't beat it! Makes the sparks fly too much! You want water. Here, give us that fork.
PRU	Where are the others? Come and help me get some water, Mr Crofton.
CROFTON	Yes... gosh, what a clot.

TOM You're too blessed late! That last shower of sparks he kicked up trying to beat the fire out's set the corn going! ... Don't waste time here, get across to The Bull as fast as your legs'll carry you and get 'em all out. We'll need everybody in sight if we're going to save this field. Pru, better nip down to Wainwright's. See if he's got any scythes – ay, or even a mower in for servicing. If we can cut a wide swathe around this lot before it spreads too far we might still save some of it. Get going, Pru, hurry. It's going up like a torch!

Unfortunately the neighbouring cornfield belonged to local grouch Percy Hood, who spent weeks trying to claim compensation off pretty much anyone he could think of. Luckily, he moved to Scotland shortly afterwards. The village was glad to see the back of him.

FIELDS OF GOLD

The colours of the countryside around Ambridge extend from green to blue and through multiple shades of yellow and gold. That's because the crops grown in the surrounding fields have evolved from wheat and barley to include peas, potatoes, sugar beet, linseed, oil seed rape to other biomass crops that convert into fuel. The colours chart the way farming has changed, with various crops falling in and out of favour.

For example, before the 1970s, the distinctive yellow hue of rapeseed was rarely seen in the English countryside. In that decade, commodity prices rose and farmers discovered that the crop attracted grants through Europe's Common Agricultural Policy. Soon the summer countryside was dazzling and farmers like Brian Aldridge, who hailed from the flat fields of Cambridgeshire, were quickly converted to its merits. Phil Archer – a man who favoured mixed farming above agricultural fads – took some convincing:

BRIAN Well, Phil, what's the verdict?

PHIL It's fascinating, Brian.

BRIAN Surprised you haven't seen rape harvested before.

PHIL I've never seriously thought of growing it myself until now. I see you've got a special attachment on the combine.

BRIAN	Must have, when this stuff grows up to six foot it has to be cut vertically as well as horizontally. An ordinary combine would never do.
PHIL	Is that attachment your own?
BRIAN	Yes, I had a fair acreage of rape at my last place. It seemed a good investment.
PHIL	Well, it does the work very efficiently.
BRIAN	And it's available for hire.
PHIL	Ha, now wait a minute. I'm only here as a bystander. I'm not going to grow rape on over half my acreage on the strength of one demonstration.
BRIAN	I'm not pushing the crop, it sells itself.
PHIL	Yes, Ralph [Bellamy] always used to say that.
BRIAN	I'm surprised he didn't grow more of it.
PHIL	Well, I think he kept meaning to. It is an interesting crop.

AMBRIDGE ANIMALS

The world of farming was changing fast in the 1950s but animal behaviour still showed familiar patterns, as Dan observed:

DAN	There's always one boss cow in any herd. One that has to rule the roost, same as among your hens.
DORIS	Works the other way with my hens... there's always one poor hen who's the victim... they always seem to pick on one...
DAN	Ah but if you take that one out and put her by herself, you'll find they'll only choose another one to be a scapegoat for all of 'em.

HORSE AND HOUND

The lives of the Archers – in common with just about everyone else they know – have been inextricably linked with the animals they love the best. From childhood most have been at home in the saddle, whether it be on the back of a waddling pony or a proud hunter. Back on terra firma there is usually a dog at their heels, that is by turns a source of delight or anguish.

Bartleby	Joe Grundy's trusty steed, at the centre of some of the Grundy money-making enterprises.
Blossom and Boxer	After Dan Archer replaced his Shire horses with a tractor, Blossom was put out to grass and Boxer was sold to Walter Gabriel.
Comet	Helen Archer's pony who died of laminitis a year after she got him, probably caused by eating too much lush pasture.
Cranford Crystal	Nigel Pargetter's heavy horse, used for bringing his coffin by cart to the parish church at Lower Loxley.
Grey Silk	The racehorse accepted by Jack Woolley in lieu of a debt.
Maisie	Caroline's 40th birthday present from her first husband Guy.
Midnight	Christine Archer's mare, whose panicked response to the stable fire in 1955 prompted Grace Archer to dash into a burning building, with fatal consequences.
Monarch	Ridden by Christine's first husband Paul Johnson.

Moonbeam	The skewbald pony bought by Brian for Debbie in 1976, the foundation of a strong stepfather-daughter relationship.
Pension	Lilian's pony when she was young.
Red Knight	The horse Lilian rode when she was married to Ralph Bellamy.
Red Link	Christine Archer's horse, actually ridden at Badminton in April 1957.
Rustic Oak, aka Ippy	Caroline's dark bay gelding, who replaced Ivor after he was put down in 1990. Three years later Ippy was stolen.
Topper	Nigel's hunter who dumped son Freddie out of the saddle.
Windermere Star	The frisky mare which kicked Chris Carter in the chest as he shoed her, landing him in Intensive Care.

Butch	Walter's dog who bit one of three youths caught setting fire to a barn on the Grenville estate in 1961.
Charlie	The spaniel puppy given to Nelson by Jack Woolley in 1989.
Gyp	The dog owned by roadman Zebedee Tring.
Gyp	Inherited by Clarrie Grundy after Jethro died in 1987, along with £5,000.
Hermes	The runt of Portia's litter taken by Lynda Snell.
Jacko	Joe's dog shot by Dan Archer in 1975 for sheep worrying.
Jet	Phil's sheepdog, who unearthed the corpse of a badger shot by David Archer in 1995.
Nell	Dan Archer's sheepdog, who died in an illegal snare at Brian's estate.

Portia	Marjorie Antrobus's Afghan hound paired from pedigree breeding with Little Croxley Owen Glendower in 1987. Unfortunately, while that coupling failed, an unscheduled meeting with Captain, the Staffordshire bull terrier belonging to Jack Woolley, was fruitful.
Tig	The sheepdog puppy that brought a delighted Freddie Pargetter to Brookfield in 2011 after his mum Elizabeth and Uncle David had fallen out.

FIELDS OF BLOOD

Lurking and silent horrors are poised to strike the farming community and catch even the most vigilant farmer unawares. Those in Ambridge, like those elsewhere, saw their animals perish in droves in distressing circumstances that were generally outside their immediate control. It's a brutal business when pens are filled with ailing animals and stock that's been tended for months or years is reduced to a pile of carcasses.

In 2001, Britain was paralysed by an outbreak of foot-and-mouth disease which cost the lives of an estimated 10 million cattle and sheep. At Brookfield David declared a state of siege to fend off the worst effects of the outbreak. But this was not the first time the spectre of foot-and-mouth had haunted the farm.

In 1956, Dan Archer was heartbroken when all cloven-footed animals were destroyed after the disease was diagnosed and Brookfield was cast into isolation. A policeman stood at the farm gate to prevent anyone entering – or leaving. It was enough to make Doris and Dan consider giving up farming, a rogue thought that has reverberated down the generations at critical times like these. This outbreak was caused when some raw liver was put in the pig swill. Happily for Dan, the slaughtered Shorthorn cows were replaced with Friesians, an altogether more productive breed.

In 2001, it was confirmation of a case at nearby Lower Croxley that sent the farm into lockdown. Pip couldn't go to school, Ruth couldn't sleep, David couldn't keep a civil tongue in his head, Phil was frustrated at not being able to do more and Jill was busy keeping the home fires burning.

One of the unsung heroes was farmworker Bert Fry, who gave up domestic joys to live in seclusion with David and Ruth. He was happy to care for the animals and help keep the dreaded disease at bay but he sorely missed Freda, her cooking and his home comforts. It was the longest they had spent apart in forty years of marriage. His only comfort came in the form of food parcels left by his loyal wife outside the farm boundaries.

Nor could he tend his beloved vegetable patch or attend the Easter quiz at The Bull. Heroically, Joe stepped in as temporary gardener. And six weeks of self-imposed segregation ended with a visit to the pub.

David Archer is notorious for his antipathy towards badgers and the threat he believes they pose to cattle with the transmission of TB. But he's not the only Ambridge farmer who has wanted to export the black and white beasts out of Ambridge in the form of sporrans.

In 1982, one of Mike Tycher's Ayrshire herd registered as a TB carrier. He and Betty had to go for TB screening as both enjoyed the unpasteurised milk produced on their farm. Things looked bleak for any badgers within a one-kilometre radius of Mike's farm when the pests officer embarked on an exhaustive hunt for infected animals. However, further investigations proved a cow previously bought and sold by Mike was the disease-carrying culprit.

In 1995, it was Brookfield Farm living with TB tensions. Bed and breakfast guests were so alarmed by the thought of it they refused to complete their stay. Then there was the cost of extra feed as none of the cows or calves were allowed off the farm except for slaughter, until the all clear. It was enough to dispatch Phil into low spirits, with a tenth of the herd likely TB suspects and badgers were firmly in the frame as carriers.

Three years later, the spectre of the disease rose again. There was no doubt that this time it was recently bought cattle that were to blame. Still, David secretly harboured the notion that vengeful badgers were trying to end farming activities at Brookfield once and for all.

One of Tony's cows contracted BSE – better known as Mad Cow disease – in 1989 and had to be destroyed. But it was Brian who came off worse in the crisis when, in the same year, he was kicked by one of Joe Grundy's infected cows. Fears that he may have contracted something far greater than a purple bruise were rife when the resulting head injury led to post-traumatic epilepsy, but ultimately more damage was done to the local economy by the outbreak than to this robust farmer.

Widespread in Britain, Johne's disease went under the radar at Brookfield Farm in 2011 as David was distracted by helping out at Lower Loxley. It's something like tuberculosis and results in thin, baleful cows with low milk yields.

Health Minister Edwina Currie whipped up a storm in 1988 when she warned the British public to beware of eggs which, she said, were pretty much riddled with salmonella. The claim was fraught with difficulties and cost the politician her job. But there was a troubling spike in the incidence of a particularly dangerous strain of salmonella.

By 1990, the salmonella shadow loomed large for Neil Carter when swabs taken as a matter of course for the ministry revealed evidence of infection. An experienced hen-keeper, he suddenly found he could not sell the 50 dozen eggs he produced daily.

Moreover, when the type of salmonella was finally identified, he was compelled to slaughter his flock. After (twice) cleaning his henhouses, he got another 1,000 birds to replace those he'd had killed, but his enthusiasm was severely dampened.

The peril of sheep scab looms when sheep haven't been treated properly against it. When David spotted Joe Grundy dousing his sheep with a water can in 1991 instead of dipping them, he was so furious that he notified Trading Standards who duly swooped on Grange Farm. The upshot was a £2,000 fine for an outraged Joe, with £200 costs. To add insult to injury, the rules were changed a year later and dipping was no longer compulsory.

In 1975, Phil happened on the symptoms of erysipelas in his pigs, also known as diamond skin disease. Notoriously tricky to diagnose, he only spotted the signs because two pigs fought after Neil, the new pigman, accidentally left pen gates open. The pigs were vaccinated before the disease got a hold of the herd.

New Forest eye, probably the most common disease found in cows, revealed itself at Willow Farm in 1974. When Tony saw the cattle with conjunctivitis he was in no doubt about what was affecting his animals.

In the same year, swine vesicular disease – with symptoms heart-stoppingly similar to foot-and-mouth disease – manifested itself at Hollowtree Farm. The disease had been appearing on farms up and down Britain for three years.

Four years later, Joe's cows were slaughtered having contracted brucellosis and he was duly compensated by the ministry.

There were other less apparent animal killers at large in Ambridge. In 1973, Jolly, one of the bull calves at Brookfield, died after having a fit. Phil later discovered it had suffered lead poisoning.

Although classical swine flu occurred in Ambridge in 1953, this highly contagious viral disease was mostly eradicated in Britain by 1966.

As disaster piled up on catastrophe for the Grundys in 1999 bovine virus diarrhoea, or BVD, was diagnosed in 65 per cent of their dairy herd, a common problem in the UK which results in reproductive problems and perpetual low-grade health issues.

Then there are crop exterminators at large in Ambridge too, with grain beetles spotted in 1977 at Brookfield wrecking £4,000 worth of wheat. Unusually, it was Peggy rather than a farmer who spotted signs of potato blight in 1990 – the same disease that caused the Irish potato famine. In 2002 the ominous grey shades of botrytis, a destructive mould, were found on the rape crop.

RE-BOAR-BATIVE

Rumours of countryside 'big cats' will never go away, but since its own reputed lynx and then a plague of wild mink in the 1980s, Ambridge seems to have specialised in wild boar.

1999

Spotted by:	Marjorie Antrobus and Hayley, out walking with Marjorie's Afghans and baby Phoebe
Later seen by:	William Grundy
Boar progeny:	A litter of Neil's Old Spot pigs with mysterious dark stripes
Photographic evidence:	To some consternation in the village, Eddie announced he was going to shoot the animal – though this turned out to be on video. Lying in wait in the woods, Eddie saw nothing, heard something, panicked, and ended up flat on his face in the mud.
The fight to the death:	Finally rejecting the idea of building a boar pit, Eddie gathered a gang of braves to track the beast. Mike, Neil and David retreated to the pub, leaving Eddie to come (so he claimed) face to face with the boar. No one believed him.

2012

Spotted by:	Scruff the Alsatian Cross, out walking with Lynda and Jim
Later seen (possibly) by:	Jazzer McCreary and Keith Horrobin
Boar progeny:	Eddie's 'Beast of Ambridge' statue – a mutant combination of two of his existing garden ornaments 'roughed up a bit'
Photographic evidence:	Lynda and Kirsty eagerly viewed CCTV from a camera left in the woods but the only activity was Nic and Will getting frisky in the great outdoors…
The fight to the death:	Eddie ran into the beast, which stove in the front of his van and led to a freezer full of unwanted boar meat at Keeper's Cottage. Eddie consoled himself with the fact that he could still market his 'Beast of Ambridge' grotesques – boldly claiming that the boar must have been being chased by something to run into the road…

ADAPT AND SURVIVE

Home Farm leads the field for farm diversifications, with the fishing lake, riding course, venison and soft fruits, but when the buzz around diversification started, it was Brookfield that was in the vanguard – or rather Jill, with her idea for farmhouse B and Bs.

Phil had always needed some convincing about the plan, but Jill forged ahead nonetheless, undeterred even when a bedside table stripped by Kenton, who was then in the antiques business, promptly fell apart and Bert Fry hung the guest bedroom wallpaper upside down. Jill rose to the challenge of a succession of visitors and their requests for vegetarian sausages, cotton sheets, high chairs and gluten-free diets, but they did nothing to win Phil over. At the time he was on the waiting list for a hip replacement, so sleep was hard to come by anyway, and when a couple with a crying baby arrived in the summer of 1991, he snapped.

He decamped to the bungalow, where Ruth and David were living, and staged a sit-in there for a whole ten days. Finally, Ruth, seeking to move on her own non-paying-guest, separately arranged to meet Phil and Jill on Lakey Hill – and then didn't turn up herself. Once they'd got over their indignation at being set up, Phil and Jill settled down to talk...

JILL I remember the first time you brought me up here. After you brought me to Brookfield to meet your mum and dad.

PHIL You thought Mum was looking you up and down all the time.

JILL She was.

PHIL And I got jealous because I thought Jack was flirting with you.

JILL He was.

PHIL He flirted with every woman.

JILL That was why I didn't mind. (BEAT) Sometimes I see him in Kenton...

They went on to talk about all the children and Jill's need to worry about them even though they were now adults. This inevitably led to reminiscences about earlier times:

JILL Do you remember when David was five and decided to run away from home?

PHIL Oh yes! Packed his little bag and walked to the bus stop on the village green.

JILL And when you brought him back he was in such a sulk for three days he wouldn't call us Mum and Dad – just Mr and Mrs Archer! (BOTH LAUGH) (BEAT)

PHIL	Can I come home again please, Mrs Archer?
JILL	(CHOKED WITH TEARS) Oh Phil! What have we been thinking about?
PHIL	I don't know about you, but I've been thinking I wish I could go home.
JILL	Then why didn't you, you... silly man?
PHIL	I don't know, pride I suppose.
JILL	I promise not to be too busy to have time for you.
PHIL	You'll let Freda Fry do more in the house?
JILL	With pleasure!

Phil went on to explain the real reason he resented the guests so much – in a way Jill could not resist.

PHIL	The thing I like about being alone in the house with you, now that the children are all grown up is it makes me realise why I married you in the first place.
JILL	Oh Phil... sometimes...
PHIL	Sometimes what?
JILL	Sometimes, you do say the sweetest things.

(POLY) TUNNEL OF LOVE

The most romantic use of an agricultural structure ever? The sound of the breeze gently playing on the crackling plastic of a polytunnel was the backdrop to Adam's first kiss with Ian Craig – now his civil partner. But the strawberry field was also where Adam's settled home life nearly began to unravel when he found himself mending a tear in the polythene late one summer evening with one of his team of pickers, the attractive and (as it turned out) manipulative Pawel.

Pawel's youthful idealism struck a chord with Adam, then battling with his conscience and stepfather Brian over the mega-dairy plans. After a disagreement with Ian, Adam spent an ill-advised night with Pawel, but when he told the young Pole it had been a mistake, Pawel forged a separate friendship with Ian. This made him a frequent visitor to Honeysuckle Cottage, which hardly helped Adam's guilty conscience. His sigh of relief when Pawel went back to Poland at the end of the season without spilling the beans could be heard in Penny Hassett. But if polytunnels could talk…

A MAN FOR ALL SEASONS

Is Brian Aldridge hero or villain, hard nut, soft touch or unscrupulous cad? With many facets to his character, the answer is probably, all of the above. When it comes to business he is coldly calculating and considers himself first among equals. Yet faced with his children he can be like butter. Well, butter that's just come out of the fridge at any rate.

He's best known for his philandering over the years. More of that later. But who remembers that he offered wife-to-be Jenny a form of pre-nup when he proposed. It was perhaps lucky for him that she refused. 'I want to marry you, not 1500 acres. Let's take it as it comes, not draw up partnership agreements,' she said. One can only speculate how many times she has regretted that down the years.

He was at his most gooey when he gave Jenny six Jacob's lambs, the kind of quirky flock disparaged by most self-respecting farmers. Those acquainted with country ways knew it was a significant symbol of his love.

There have been other promising signs of his inner goodness since then – but that self-serving side of his nature is always somewhere in the shadows.

When a new wood for the new millennium was mooted in 1998, Phil and David debated the idea of donating a strip of Brookfield land – but it came to nothing. It was Brian who stepped in with the five acres, which have since been planted up with saplings, among them oak and a 'year-round colour mixture', as well as sheltering a picnic site and bluebell glade.

The fact that he and Jennifer had originally hoped the wood could be named the Aldridge Millennium Wood and would provide cover for the shoot (vetoed by the Woodland Trust who have the 199-year lease) is something they kept to themselves.

Funnily enough, Brian didn't seem as keen for his name to be attached to the plot when it became the Ambridge Natural Burial Site. Though he'd deny to his dying day that he only gave the land as a sweetener to pacify Lynda Snell over the diversion of a footpath to make way for an extension to the polytunnels ('Nonsense – it's called corporate social responsibility, Jenny!'), his wife recognises the truth.

Jill was not so compliant when Brian offered Borchester Land's sponsorship for the village's Britain in Bloom efforts. She knew all too well it was just a public-relations stunt to try to smooth the passage of his mega-dairy plans. She carefully sidestepped the offer.

The unsentimental streak which largely defines him in both tender and tough moments comes even more readily to the fore these days. Reluctantly, he toured the Grundys' farm in 1986 when its historic value was being trumpeted:

JENNY	It's such a lovely old building this. Some of it dates back to the Middle Ages.
BRIAN	The barn I expect. Wattle and daub and plastic sheeting – very traditional.

JENNY	That wall was once part of the monastery.
BRIAN	And what about Eddie's old motorbike? Did that get a mention in the Domesday Book?

The same year he was proud to say that Home Farm had no otters and few hedges within its boundaries.

When it came to the Open Farm Day being held at Brookfield Farm in 2010 Brian had character-revealing words for Gerry Morton, a fellow director of Borchester Land.

BRIAN	They are going for it in a big way. We are just lending them our combine for the great unwashed to gawp at.
GERRY	Steady, Brian.
BRIAN	Sorry, to help bring about a greater understanding of agriculture amongst our revered consumers and taxpayers.

WORK EXPERIENCE

Phil was a farmer, born and bred. But Grace, his awfully well-brought-up fiancée was more about couture and manicures than chickens. Nonetheless, she was game in offering to help Phil with his flock.

PHIL — I'm also culling a few of these birds. You can do it if you like, Grace. You've only got to wring their necks.

GRACE — Heavens, no!

PHIL — I'll have to do it myself then.

GRACE — Why do you wring their necks?

PHIL — To... kill them, sweetie.

GRACE — No, you amaze me. Now that's what I call a most instructive answer.

PHIL — Oh, I get you. You mean, why do I kill them?

GRACE — Yes.

PHIL — Well, you see, their laying days are ended and we can't afford to keep them when they are like that. They take good grub and they show nothing for it. We don't just feed them for the pleasure of having them around the place, you know.

GRACE — Gosh. Lucky for us the human race isn't governed by the same rules.

THE END OF THE ROAD

In farming as in other industries, bankruptcies are an occupational hazard. Mike Tucker went bust at Ambridge Farm, as did Christine Barford's first husband, Paul Johnson, when his fish farm failed. Tom Archer was almost bankrupt before he was rescued by his uncle Brian after his contract with a supermarket chain was abruptly terminated, while Robert Snell's computer business fell apart in the mid-1990s.

£

The village's most notorious bankrupt was probably former Estate owner Cameron Fraser, who persuaded people as diverse as Caroline Bone and Marjorie Antrobus to invest in his fraudulent speculations. Phil Archer never liked him (and rightly so – who would trust a man who wore white socks, installed gold taps in the Dower House and always ordered the swankiest bottle of wine on the list?) but Phil's daughter Elizabeth, who was going out with Cameron, was blind to these and his many other faults.

She stood by her lover, only seeing through him when he abandoned her, pregnant, at a café off the motorway en route to what she thought was a get-away-from-it-all holiday in the sun. The only person who got away, however, was Fraser.

Through everyone else's vicissitudes, somehow, incredibly, Joe Grundy, and then his son Eddie, managed to cling on as tenants at Grange Farm. Scraping a living, borrowing other people's equipment (even trying to re-use Brookfield's sheep dip on one occasion), ducking and diving from one money-making scheme to the next (which never did make money) they endured for years.

But come the new millennium, new Estate owners Borchester Land and a bank which refused to extend their credit, the Grundys' time was finally up. There was to be a farm sale on the premises and an unlucky chap named Waring was sent out from the auctioneers to value the dead and livestock. Understandably he was met by a bitter Eddie, who scrutinised his every move:

WARING	Look, we're just going to be putting up our ring. Sticking on lot numbers. That sort of thing. You don't really want to see that.
EDDIE	Too right I do… I'll tell you, mate, I'm going to be following you about like sheep ticks on a dog fox. So you'd better get used to it.

Later, as threatened, Eddie found Waring in the yard, being, 'creative in our lotting up' – such as putting a breeding chart in with an old slurry pump in the hope of attracting a few bids. Eddie was sceptical:

EDDIE And what about all them hand tools? The hay rakes and pitch forks? Who's going to buy that sort of stuff?

WARING They'll go all right. No trouble at all. The heritage industry. It seems to be insatiable.

EDDIE (CONTEMPT) Oh, heritage. Is that it?

WARING You've seen these theme pubs. They're always on the lookout for genuine artefacts.

EDDIE Funny, ain't it? It wasn't many years ago they wanted every last bit of food we could turn out. Now all they want is heritage...

WARING Let me give you a piece of advice, Mr Grundy. Try not to look on this experience as a disaster. Try to see it as an opportunity. A chance to make a fresh start...

EDDIE Great. I'll go and put it on my CV. Maybe they'll give me a smock and a pitchfork and stick me in a museum: British Farmer – extinct.

Ouch. But Waring still had a long day ahead of him, and a job to do, and Eddie wasn't finished with him. Again, it was an old hand tool that set him off:

EDDIE	See them initials? There, look...
WARING	Yes.
EDDIE	G.G. Shall I tell you who that was? George Grundy. My dad's father. My granddad. And you see how it's all worn down round the base? Any idea how it got like this?
WARING	From repeated use I imagine?
EDDIE	That's right. Work. Pitching up hundreds of tons of hay ten foot up on the back of a cart. Then pitching it off again on the elevator. Summer after summer. Year after year. To keep twenty pedigree Dairy Shorthorns in milk...
WARING	I appreciate it's got a history.
EDDIE	And I'll tell you where that milk used to go. Out on the streets of Borchester to feed poor little beggars whose mums didn't have the money to put boots on their feet. And I'll tell you sommat else. It didn't matter a toss to them folks if they stuck antique hay rakes on the pub wall or if they didn't. Just so long as their little 'uns never had rickets.
WARING	I think you've made your point, Mr Grundy.

EDDIE	This lot's coming with me. (TOOLS GATHERED UP) You can stuff your Lot 33A.
WARING	I'll mark it withdrawn.
EDDIE	You do that. And you can tell them money-grubbing vultures you work for. One of these days when they've put the last little farmer out of business, this country's going to go hungry again. Only it'll be too blimming late. And who'll be sorry then?

When the time came to leave Grange Farm, it was a limpid April evening. William, who was to lodge with his godmother Caroline so he could carry on his job as a gamekeeper, was at the farm to see the family off. Ed had gone on ahead to their new home, a cramped flat on the notorious Borchester council estate at Meadow Rise.

CLARRIE	(APP, WITH CLANKING MOP AND BUCKET) Here you are, Eddie, that's the lot.
EDDIE	You've never been cleaning?
CLARRIE	(TIGHT) I just gave the kitchen floor one last going over.
EDDIE	You must be barmy.
CLARRIE	I wanted to.
WILLIAM	Give it here, Mum. (MOP AND BUCKET STOWED IN VAN)

EDDIE	Is that the lot? Dad?
JOE	I ain't got nothing.
EDDIE	(SLAMS BACK DOOR OF VAN) Right. (PAUSE) Well. (AT A LOSS) We might as well go then.
CLARRIE	I suppose so. (BEAT) Do you... do you want to lock up, Joe?
JOE	No. You do it, Clarrie.
CLARRIE	All right then. (GOES TO BACK DOOR) (ALL STAND SILENT AS CLARRIE LOCKS BACK DOOR, OFF A BIT. SKYLINE. THEN:)
WILLIAM	(GENTLE) Come on, Granddad. In you get...

As if that wasn't bad enough, before they could go there was a further twist of the knife. Brookfield had agreed to look after the Grundys' collie, Tess, as pets weren't allowed at Meadow Rise. But:

CLARRIE	I'll pop by and see you after work tomorrow, William.
WILLIAM	OK. (BARKING OF RUNNING COLLIE, OFF)
EDDIE	(SELF) Oh blimey.
CLARRIE	Oh it's not –
WILLIAM	Tess. She's come back.
EDDIE	That's all we need. (MORE BARKS, APP)

WILLIAM Look, you go. I'll take her back to Brookfield.

CLARRIE I don't like to –

WILLIAM You haven't got time.

EDDIE Come on, Clarrie, love, Edward'll be walking the streets.

CLARRIE All right then. (DOG NOW ON, BARKS)

EDDIE (PATS DOG) That's it, Tess. Hello, girl.

CLARRIE Oh dear. Oh dear. Bye William. (GOES A BIT, GETS IN VAN. DOOR SLAMS)

WILLIAM Bye, Mum. Bye, Dad.

EDDIE (SLAPS WILLIAM ON BACK, EMOTIONAL) Cheerio, son. (PATS DOG) Ta-ra, Tess old girl. (EDDIE GOES A BIT, GETS IN VAN. DOOR SLAMS)

WILLIAM (CROUCHES BY DOG) Come on then, Tess. Good dog, aren't you? Yes. (ENGINE STARTS) That's it, good girl. Stay. (VAN MOVES OFF) (CALLS, WAVING) Bye! (TESS WHINES) It's no good, Tess. You don't live here any more. None of us does. (THE VAN RECEDES)

LOVE LIFE

THEY SAY THE PATH of true love rarely runs smoothly and that's never more accurate than when the bumpy farm tracks of Ambridge are involved. Ambridge has had more than its fair share of secret assignations and raunchy rendezvous for old and young alike. Certainly, it's a place where the adage 'love thy neighbour' is sometimes taken far too literally. Thankfully, the village has its fair share of dewy-eyed romance too, with an abundance of proposals between loving couples.

If soft lighting and violins is absent, genuine strength of feeling is not, and it is this that brings a tear unbidden to the eye. Sometimes it is a case of love rather than marriage, and the tradition of producing a love child begun by Jennifer Archer in 1967 has continued down the decades.

Remarkably she is now mother to Ruairi, a child produced from the love affair between husband Brian and Siobhan Donovan, deceased. Indeed, Brian's other dalliances were flippant things compared to the intense relationship he struck up with Siobhan. It was this coupling that proved the most significant challenge to an otherwise surprisingly sturdy marriage.

Not everyone in Ambridge has been as adept as Brian at wooing and winning. In fact, Phil Archer has been an outright failure and Jill was no doubt grateful for the fact he was an 'also ran' in the affairs stakes. With Pat and Tony Archer tempted to stray at times during their long marriage there's plenty of proof that it is unfeasibly hard to stay happily wed. Meanwhile some relationships, illicit or otherwise, end in tears and consequently bring boot-black heartbreak to even the happiest souls.

AND SO TO… WED

On bended knee at the top of the Eiffel Tower, at sunset on a secluded beach, or the old engagement ring in the glass of champagne trick? No such romantic clichés for the impassioned of Ambridge. The men – and occasionally women – driven to propose have sometimes gone for full-frontal romance; sometimes the moment has been more humdrum. But for the happy couple, doubtless the moment was equally memorable, whatever.

ALAN FRANKS TO USHA GUPTA

Alan had planned a romantic walk in Borchester's riverside park but, foiled by the attentions of first a homeless person and then a busker, ended up proposing in the car park as Usha hurried to get back to work.

PHIL ARCHER TO JILL PATERSON

Phil first stated his intentions in September 1957 as Jill's train pulled out of New Street Station in Birmingham. They'd only known each other a few weeks.

JILL	Bye. (LEANS IN, KISS ON CHEEK)
PHIL	You're not getting away with just a peck. Not when I'm going to miss you as much as I am.
JILL	I know. (BEAT) I have to go. (CLIMBS ONTO TRAIN, DOOR SLAMS, WINDOW LOWERED) Don't forget to write. (WHISTLE BLOWS, TRAIN BEGINS TO MOVE)
PHIL	(WALKS, THEN JOGS, ALONGSIDE TRAIN) I won't. And don't forget you're going to marry me.
JILL	(ASTONISHED) Am I?

She did put up a bit of a fight, at first telling Phil, 'I could never be a farmer's wife' and trying to claim she was a city girl at heart. But Phil fought back, telling her 'everyone has roots in the country' and, after a visit to Ambridge and a crayfish supper, Jill saw sense. By November 1957, they were married and twins Kenton and Shula – honeymoon babies – were born just nine months later.

CHRIS CARTER TO ALICE ALDRIDGE

Now this was a romantic location, overlooking the Grand Canyon, as a besotted Alice told her startled parents, who were still reeling from the revelation that the pair, supposedly simply on holiday in America, had married in the wedding chapel in Las Vegas:

ALICE	(DREAMY) I'll never forget what he said.
CHRIS	What did I say?
ALICE	'Alice, will you marry me?'
BRIAN	Well, that's original, anyway.

Brian later recovered enough to counsel Jennifer to think of it as 'a starter marriage' – but the worst was yet to hit Jennifer when she realised: 'I'm related to a Horrobin!'

IAN CRAIG TO ADAM MACY

Four years earlier, Brian had had even more of a shock when Adam announced he was engaged:

JENN	How did you get on last night?
ADAM	Ah, well...
BRIAN	Oh yes, you were going to see that Italian bloke, weren't you?

ADAM	Yes. Only he wasn't Italian after all. He was Ian.
BRIAN	What?
ADAM	AC Ragini. It's an anagram of his name.
BRIAN	But why should Ian summon you halfway across the county to talk about Hassett Hills venison?
ADAM	He didn't. That was just a ploy to get me to the restaurant.
JENN	A surprise party?
ADAM	Well... it was certainly a surprise. The place is run by a friend of his, and we had this gorgeous meal.
JENN	Oh, how sweet.
ADAM	And then he proposed.
JENN	What?
ADAM	He asked me to marry him.
JENN	Oh darling!
BRIAN	Marry him?
JENN	How lovely! Did you say yes?
ADAM	Of course. He gave me this ring.
JENN	Oh, isn't that beautiful!
BRIAN	(INWARDLY APPALLED) You can't marry him!
ADAM	Why not?
BRIAN	Because... you and him...

JENN — Oh darling, don't split hairs. It may not be called marriage, it's called a civil partnership, but it amounts to the same thing.

BRIAN — No, it doesn't.

JENN — So when's it going to be, the wedding?

BRIAN — Wedding?

ADAM — We haven't fixed the date yet.

JENN — But you're not just going to sneak down to the registry office?

ADAM — Oh no, we thought we'd have a bit of a do.

BRIAN — A do?

ADAM — Somewhere like Grey Gables or Lower Loxley. We can write our own vows, and choose some nice music, and bits of poetry.

JENN — And you'll have a proper reception, with champagne, and a cake?

ADAM — (SMILE) Of course. Don't look so alarmed, Brian. I'm not going to ask you to give me away.

PAT LEWIS TO TONY ARCHER

Pat's never been afraid to speak her mind, and it was no different when she proposed to Tony on 25 October 1974. 'Marry me, Tony Archer!' she commanded. And, Reader, within two months, he had.

MARK HEBDEN TO SHULA ARCHER

This didn't start well. In late 1980, Mark defended a pair of hunt saboteurs, Mr and Mrs Jarrett, when they appeared before Borchester magistrates accused of causing a breach of the peace, with Mrs Jarrett further accused of spray-painting a fencepost. After a guilty verdict was handed down, Mark, in an ill-advised quote to the *Echo*, called the magistrates 'socially accepted amateurs' who 'represented the bias of a Borchester high-class Mafia' – bad enough on its own, but worse, far worse, when Phil, his girlfriend's father, was the bench's Chair. Mark appealed the guilty verdict and got it overturned, and Phil later accepted Mark's apology for what he'd said to the paper, though he didn't think it sounded very sincere: 'Sounded as though he was making a speech at court – you know – spur of the moment, deeply regret, all that sort of thing.' Mark was invited to the Brookfield New Year's Eve party nevertheless, where he was keen to make amends. As Jill noted: 'He's definitely on his best behaviour. He's thanked me three times for asking him.' But as midnight approached, Mark contrived to get himself on his own with Shula…

SHULA	Well, aren't I going to get a kiss for the New Year?
MARK	No, not for a minute.
SHULA	Oh, thanks very much. (PAUSE) Do you want to say it's not going to work out again? I mean, I know my dad's a bit cross with you at the moment, but that doesn't mean we can't go out together, does it?
MARK	No.
SHULA	Well, what are you looking so glum about?
MARK	(DEEP BREATH) I wanted to ask you something.
SHULA	(CHEERFUL) Fire ahead.
MARK	What do you think about me?
SHULA	What do I...? Well, I think you're very nice. I like you, I like you very much.
MARK	Do you love me?
SHULA	Do you love me?
MARK	I asked you first.
SHULA	I – might. But only if you love me.
MARK	Oh, that's all right. I do. Very much.
SHULA	(SMILE) Now can I have a kiss?
MARK	Well – there was something else.
SHULA	Oh?
MARK	Would you like to marry me?
SHULA	Marry you? You mean – get married?
MARK	Yes.

SHULA	(PAUSE) Was that a proposal?
MARK	Yes.
SHULA	That's the first one I've ever had.
MARK	(SLIGHTLY IMPATIENT) Shula –
SHULA	It's a bit of a surprise – I mean I wasn't expecting it – yes, I will!
MARK	(MAKING SURE) You will marry me?
SHULA	Yes, if you want to. Yes, definitely. Shall we go and tell everyone?
MARK	Hang on, Shula – you can have that kiss now.

It will come as no surprise to hear that Shula was not, in fact, ready to get married, to Mark or anyone else, and their planned wedding did not take place – at least not immediately. It was another five years before they finally realised they were right for each other after all. They married on 21 September 1985.

OLIVER STERLING TO CAROLINE PEMBERTON

Who'd have thought that Oliver's stiff upper exterior concealed the beating heart of a true romantic? But he went to the trouble of creating a magical setting when he proposed to Caroline in 2006, filling the terrace with dozens of roses and entwining fairy lights in the climbers on the trellis before proposing over a glass of champagne.

BERT HORROBIN TO IVY

As Ivy's health crumbled in 2011 under the weight of a lifetime's worry and work, she recalled how husband Bert proposed. They'd been to a dance together at the Locarno in Felpersham, with Bert proudly clad in his Teddy Boy garb. His drape coat and fancy waistcoat cost him £17 10 shillings, she remembered. He walked her home and, when they got to her doorstep, he went down on one knee asking: 'Ivy, will you do me the honour…'

'Then my mum opened the door and screamed her head off, and called inside: "Father, Bert's gonna make an honest woman out of our Ivy."'

ROY TUCKER TO HAYLEY JORDAN

Friendship turned into something very much more passionate and enduring between Roy and Hayley. Their inner feelings were unleashed with a Millennium kiss but that led to a period of awkwardness that was only overcome weeks later. This is how they proposed to take their relationship to another level.

HAYLEY	I've been thinking about you all the time, as well.
ROY	Have you?
HAYLEY	Yes.

ROY	I couldn't work out any way to tell you… well, to tell you…
HAYLEY	Tell me what?
ROY	I care about you. That sounds so weird.
HAYLEY	No it doesn't. It sounds fabulous.
ROY	You mean that?
HAYLEY	I really care about you, Roy.

Both had been going out with other people when they first met and didn't consider the other as potential partner material…

HAYLEY	Isn't it embarrassing when… when your feelings change?
ROY	Yeah. I couldn't believe it was happening.
HAYLEY	When did you notice?
ROY	What?
HAYLEY	That you felt differently.
ROY	I don't know. A while ago. I just didn't have the guts to say.
HAYLEY	I wish you had.
ROY	I couldn't admit it to myself, let alone you.

The couple eventually tied the knot on 7 May 2001.

THE ROMANCING OF MRS P

For years Walter Gabriel's slow-burning passion for the redoubtable Mrs P was unrequited. No matter. Walter was prepared to take things slowly, as this conversation with Dan Archer and farmhand Simon revealed.

It happened when the pair could not help but notice how Walter Gabriel was continually scratching his nether regions as they spoke. Both had a theory about the cause:

DAN	I reckon some corn dust must have worked its way down your trousers.
SIMON	It's not fleas, is it?
WALTER	No, I never had 'em... not in March, anyway.

In fact an 'emery paper' patch sewn into his trousers by Mrs P was apparently to blame. Love-struck Walter would not mention the itch it had given him for fear of offending her – and his only other pair of trousers was in the wash. Simon proposed a radical solution:

SIMON	If you was to marry her you could speak your mind instead of trying not to hurt her feelings.
WALTER	That's enough of that, Simon. I knew t'would start. Just cos her mends me pants you want to get us up to the altar steps at full gallop. Well, I won't gallop for nobody.

Thus Mrs P remained a firm friend rather than a femme fatale. And he lived to regret this leisurely pursuit. He presumably would have broken out into a canter if only he'd known the race was on.

Soon afterwards Mrs P – who was Peggy's mum and known to moan – was somewhat unexpectedly at the centre of a love triangle after the arrival of Arthur Perkins, who shared her surname but was no relation. He came to Ambridge at the request of the Fairbrother family to create a memorial window in the church for Grace Archer.

With Walter Gabriel waiting in the wings, it was perhaps surprising that Mrs P was hesitant to accept the proposal of a wealthy, artistic, suave, well-spoken outsider. When it finally came – as the pair took a ride in her pony and trap in 1959 – her acceptance was genteel, almost grudging, although Arthur was nonetheless bowled over.

POLLY — It would mean changing my life again. Leaving the cottage I've got fond of, leaving Peg and Jack just as they are taking over The Bull for themselves and might be glad of a bit of help. Leaving all the friends I've made, perhaps having to change my habits that I've got used to, living on my own.

PERKINS — I realise I am asking you to make an awful sacrifice. Why should you give up your independence?

POLLY	I didn't say they were sacrifices, Mr Perkins. What I said was, that they were some of the things that I would have to consider if I was changing my life again. At my age you have got to look at it practical.
PERKINS	Yes, Polly.
POLLY	Well, I've come to the conclusion I'm prepared to do it. I'll marry you, Arthur Perkins.
PERKINS	What! Oh Polly, thank you, thank you.
POLLY	All right, there's no need to make a fool of me. We're both old enough to know better.
PERKINS	You have made me very, very happy. I feel too full up to say much but I think you know.
POLLY	Mmm, I think I've known all along.
PERKINS	Really?
POLLY	Some folk you get on with and some you don't. Some you take to and like at once. I liked you, Arthur. I felt safe somehow.
PERKINS	Ah, well, this is peace at last.

She left Ambridge in a shiny new car, heading for a cruise, with the promise that this was only the beginning ringing in her ears, returning to Ambridge after the death of Mr Perkins some seven years later.

HORMONES AT HOME FARM

PLAGUED BY THE NIGHTINGALE

Received wisdom has it that it's Brian with the wandering eye but – not that it in any way justifies his subsequent behaviour – the first person to stray in their marriage was Jennifer.

In 1980, local antiques expert John Tregorran, Ambridge's nearest thing to an intellectual, suggested she join him at a series of local history lectures and a friendship burgeoned out of their shared interest. It might have stayed that way had John not decided that Ambridge itself merited investigation. He and Jennifer organised a landscape survey which gave them the excuse for hours in each other's company, much of it in secluded rural spots.

John even persuaded Jack Woolley to publish the results as a book, which then required a launch, and an exhibition of photographs in Jennifer's 'studio' at Home Farm. But if Jennifer had enjoyed the attention, and the mental stimulus, she wasn't ready for John to take things further, as he tried to, in a bluebell wood. Having first pointed out that the bluebells were an indication that it dated back to medieval times and held forth on subjects as varied as wild garlic, cuckoos, the small-leaved lime and the poetry of Edward Thomas, he turned all philosophical…

JENN	John? I don't like to see you looking so melancholy.
JOHN	I'm sorry… I was just thinking. All the things we're capable of doing in our lifetime – and how little most of us actually do.
JENN	Oh, John.
JOHN	You ought to keep on writing.
JENN	I know. But things get in the way. (CHUCKLES) Landscape Surveys – children…
JOHN	Would you like an idea?
JENN	I don't know. What's it for? Short story? Novel? … What is the idea?
JOHN	Well, it's about a man in early middle age… married for some years. He has a good marriage – very good – with a reasonably high standard of living, holidays in Brittany… the Greek islands… only he has this rather dreamy side to his nature…
JENN	A hopeless romantic, you mean?
JOHN	No, not <u>hopeless</u> – he just has this discontent… He has a life that many people would envy – he ought to be fulfilled and pleased with his situation and yet… there's a dull ache… All the time… (BEAT) Well – think you could make something of it. Jenny my love?

JENN	(PAUSE) No, John. It's not really my kind of story.
JOHN	(PAUSE) I'm sorry. I thought you might understand –
JENN	No. I'm sorry.
JOHN	You see he does have this other woman friend –
JENN	No.
JOHN	(SIGH) It doesn't interest you at all, Jenny?
JENN	Not enough, John.
JOHN	Ah. Well I suppose that old eternal triangle business is rather played out. (<u>CUCKOO CALLS</u>) Jenny…
JENN	(GOING) I'll see you tomorrow, John. We set off from The Bull, don't forget!
JOHN	But Jenny, don't run off! Hey! (SHOUTING AFTER HER) I've even got a title for it!
JENN	(FAR OFF) Bye, John.
JOHN	(CALLS) Bye… (PAUSE. <u>CUCKOO NEARER</u>) Oh be quiet, you stupid, stupid bird!
	(<u>FADE UP CUCKOO</u>)

Jennifer had made things pretty plain but in any case Brian – and John's wife, Carol – were not the sort of partners to stand by and be publicly humiliated. Brian told Jennifer flatly to stop spending so much time with John, while Carol conclusively made that happen by packing her husband off to run antique fairs in America. But that wasn't quite the end of the story for Jennifer and Brian. It was the landscape survey that first brought Caroline on to Brian's radar (literally – he flew her and Jennifer over Ambridge in a light aircraft to take aerial photographs). Caroline loved it. Jennifer was air-sick.

THEY COULD HAVE DANCED ALL NIGHT

Was it a midlife crisis or something from his past that made Brian behave like a latter-day Lothario? Perhaps it is no surprise to discover that Brian Aldridge was a lad-about-town in his younger years. The son of wealthy farmers, he spent much of his time living it up in Paris and was about to go on a skiing holiday when both his parents died in a car crash. Aged 28, he was left with a large cereal farm to run singlehandedly in Cambridgeshire. Reluctantly, he realised his jet-setting days were over, but clearly many of his wild oats were left unsown.

After their airborne encounter via the landscape survey, nothing happened romantically between Caroline and Brian until a few years later when she'd been dumped by yet another promising boyfriend. As her last two had been in the SAS and the Fleet Air Arm respectively, maybe she simply decided that a beau nearer home might be a good idea. Whatever, after they danced together at the Hunt Ball in March 1983, Caroline and Brian began an affair, initially fuelled by a shared love of good food.

BRIAN	Finish off the Fleurie. It's very good for a guilty conscience. (POURS) Jenny's perfectly happy, you know. There's no need to feel the slightest bit guilty about her.
CAROLINE	I'll be the keeper of my conscience, thank you very much.
BRIAN	Hoity-toity! But there isn't, really.
CAROLINE	I can't think what I'm doing...
BRIAN	You couldn't resist the free lunches.

When Brian's brother-in-law Tony caught them kissing behind a hedge, smooth-talking Brian brushed it off as a birthday kiss. It took guileless Tony some while to realise that Caroline's birthday had been weeks before, but Caroline's guilt soon got the better of her and she ended things. If nothing else, Shula's horrified incredulity over her friend's choice of lover – 'Brian? *Brian!*' – must have convinced her she was doing the right thing. Caroline stood firm when Brian continued to pursue her but there remained a definite frisson – on Brian's side, at least – for many years.

THICK AND FAST

Over a year after Caroline had dumped him, Brian was still not taking no for an answer and took to turning up unexpectedly wherever she might be found. When Jennifer learnt that they'd been spotted 'together' at an auction, all hell broke loose. Brian tried to claim he'd been a shoulder for Caroline to cry on after another failed romance ('Making me sound like a hopeless neurotic!' as Caroline complained to Shula) and while an uncomfortable Caroline seriously contemplated leaving the village, Brian put his energies into rebuilding things with Jennifer, even whisking her away on holiday, unheard of for a busy farmer. On the surface things calmed down, but the affair with Caroline had triggered something in Brian and by the late 1980s his roving eye was practically astigmatic.

It alighted first on red-haired horsewoman Mandy Beesborough, whom he had plenty of chance to see when taking his daughter Kate to the Pony Club.

When Jennifer found out about his interest in Mandy and protested, a make-up baby seemed to be the answer, but even while Jennifer was pregnant, Brian didn't modify his behaviour. With Mandy more or less off limits, he turned to Betty Tucker, who, after her husband Mike's farm had gone bankrupt, had become the Aldridges' cleaner. When Brian suggested they take a dip in the Home Farm swimming pool – and never mind if she didn't have a costume – Betty fled, pouring everything out to the first person she met – who, luckily, was Jill. Jill duly tore Brian off a strip but even she couldn't subdue him entirely – he was at the races with Mandy when Jennifer went into labour with baby Alice. Brian's disappointment at another daughter was tangible but in the end it was a *force majeure* which temporarily neutered him – he contracted post-traumatic epilepsy after a kick in the head from a BSE-infected cow. It would be over ten years before he strayed again.

LOVE IN THE AFTERNOON

After everything she'd suffered with Brian, it's hardly surprising that, when her ex-husband Roger Travers Macy reappeared on his daughter Debbie's 21st birthday in 1991, Jennifer might have started to wonder if she'd have been better off – emotionally at least – staying with him. An uncomfortable Jill found herself embroiled in the affair from the start, Jennifer asking Jill to provide her with an alibi for an early rendezvous with Roger and confiding that sex with him during their marriage had been wonderful. By the time Jill encountered the pair in Underwoods' Food Hall shortly after, Jennifer and Roger were shopping for a cosy post-coital picnic. But Brian had had too much experience himself not to know an affair when he saw one, while Debbie, then living at home, and Peggy, who found herself minding toddler Alice, also knew Something Was Up. Jennifer didn't help herself by inventing flimsy excuses for her absences, like shopping trips with no resultant purchases – as if! – though her hotel-room encounters with Roger poignantly revealed huge depths of vulnerability and doubt:

ROGER Anything you want from room service?

JENN Nope.

ROGER Drink? Sandwich?

JENN I just want to lie here for ever.

ROGER Still no guilt?

JENN No. Isn't that awful?

ROGER It's not good or bad. Just how it is. Perhaps it means we were right for each other.

JENN Could do.

ROGER I suppose I've always known that somewhere... For me this is like coming home.

JENN It's starting to get dark out there.

ROGER Shall I draw the curtains?

JENN No, no, not yet. I like looking at it. It doesn't seem real somehow... (PAUSE) Shall I tell you what bothers me?

ROGER If you want to.

JENN If you and I have always belonged together, what have I been doing with Brian all these years?

ROGER I thought you said no guilt?

JENN No, it's not guilt. It makes me sad, that's all.

Moved, Roger caught her in a passionate kiss, only to be interrupted by a phone call on his mobile. It was Debbie, innocently wanting to check the arrangements for her next meeting with her father. (Roger: 'I've just stepped out of the shower… can I call you back?') For him, the mood was broken – but Jennifer couldn't let go:

ROGER	I'm sorry.
JENN	It's not your fault.
ROGER	(SITS UP) I'll get dressed.
JENN	No. Don't go. Hold me. Please.

Finally, though, it was divine intervention which brought her to her senses, in the form of a reproach from her Uncle Tom. Sunday's church flowers, he said, had been a disgrace – and all because Jennifer had forgotten it was her turn on the rota. It was a telling symbol of everything she had to lose and everyone she was letting down, so Jennifer told Roger things had to stop. Brian didn't let her off the hook so easily, though, especially when poor Jennifer tried to show an interest in his fishing lake. 'It was the same with oilseed rape,' he told Debbie elliptically, 'when she'd finished that book with John Tregorran.' But an accident involving Alice and a savaged sheep gradually brought husband and wife, family and farm, back together. Their marriage had lived to fight another day, but next time it would be a fight almost to the death.

MEN WERE DECEIVERS EVER

This time it was serious – really serious – because Brian's lover, Siobhan Hathaway, fell pregnant. She'd already lost a baby by her husband, village doctor Tim, but she knew for sure that this baby was Brian's. Siobhan and Tim parted after he worked out there was another man and speculation about a clandestine relationship swirled through the village. It's hard to say who suffered greater agony when Siobhan went into labour, Brian being trapped at his mother-in-law Peggy's birthday party. But though his joy at the birth of a son was unconfined, he proved reluctant to disturb his domestic life, let alone go near the financial implications of a divorce. It was Debbie who uncovered the affair and in the most mundane way possible – when she saw Siobhan mopping up Ruairi's regurgitated milk with one of Brian's monogrammed handkerchiefs. Back at Home Farm, she waited up for her father and there was a two-in-the-morning confrontation, coloured by the fact that Debbie had only recently found out about her own husband, Simon's, infidelity, and had left him.

BRIAN	Oh, Debbie... this is the last thing I wanted...
DEB	(VERY BITTER) A bit inevitable, I should have thought. Or did you think you could get away with it for ever?
BRIAN	No, I... I don't know.
DEBBIE	So? (BIG PAUSE)

BRIAN	I never meant it to happen. It was meant to be just a fling. Not even that. I mean... in the beginning, well.... I don't quite know how it started. But her marriage was on the rocks and I suppose... I suppose she was looking for... for a bit of solace elsewhere.
DEB	So she threw herself at you, is that what you're saying?
BRIAN	No, no, no, it wasn't like that. But she was... she's a very beautiful woman. And twenty years younger than me. So when she showed an interest in me, well, I... I couldn't believe my luck, to be honest. But I really thought... I didn't think it would last. I mean, a woman like her? I thought she'd get bored, move on.
DEB	Instead of which, she got pregnant.
BRIAN	Yes. I don't know how...
DEB	The usual way, I imagine.

Debbie insisted that if Brian didn't tell Jennifer in the morning, she would. He did, and instantly, everything was up in the air.

JENN	When he started to tell me – I thought it meant the affair was over, because that's what it's meant in the past, but there's a child. This can never be over for him.
DEB	Never mind about him. What do you want, Mum?
JENN	I don't know. Everything I thought was certain – it's all gone.
DEB	Is that how you feel?
JENN	I feel numb. Twenty-seven years gone in a sentence...
DEB	So what are you going to do?
JENN	I haven't the faintest idea.

The agonies continued, not helped by the fact that it was the week before Christmas, with all the pressures that brings. Behind the public facade of attending the village Christmas show, and giving Home Farm's own Christmas party, there were parallel encounters for Brian with both the women in his life:

JENN	Do you love her?
BRIAN	(FATAL PAUSE) Well –
JENN	You do, don't you?
BRIAN	I love you too, darling. I do.
JENN	Do you?
BRIAN	Yes!
JENN	That's unfortunate, Brian. Because you can't have both of us, can you?

And:

SIOBHAN	You could be here with us.
BRIAN	Oh, Siobhan.
SIOBHAN	But you're clinging to your old life, and I can't see any reason for that, unless – Brian, do you still love Jennifer? (FATAL PAUSE) Look at me. Do you still love Jennifer? (PAUSE)
BRIAN	Siobhan –
SIOBHAN	Oh my God. You do, don't you?
BRIAN	I love you too. You know how much I love you. You and the baby.
SIOBHAN	You can't have all of us, Brian. Not any more.

After much agonising, Brian elected to stay with Jennifer, and Siobhan took Ruairi first to Ireland and then to Germany, where she worked as a translator. Brian had minimal contact with his son, but Siobhan had a last tragic card to play, turning up without warning in 2007 to announce that she had terminal cancer. Brian had more work to do with Jennifer to persuade her that they should provide a home for Ruairi, but with superhuman strength and compassion, she agreed, and has, as Brian has the grace to acknowledge, made a superb job of it. However, she makes sure to avoid the Millennium Wood's Siobhan Hathaway Memorial Picnic Area, so called in Jennifer's mind because there's a bench there which Ruairi knows is in memory of his mother.

AN AFFAIR TO… FORGET

TONY ARCHER AND LIBBY JONES

'Hello, Tony… I've come to measure your milk yield…' What red-blooded man could resist an offer like that? Certainly not Tony Archer in the summer of 1977, when West Country siren Elizabeth (Libby) Jones began working as the MMB's milk recorder in the Ambridge district. By the evening of the cricket club dance, he was brazening it out to Jennifer with a killer line of his own: 'I'd bought a double ticket… It seemed mad to waste it.' Tony's always been thrifty but his sister wasn't buying this excuse for a moment – not with Pat away, having taken her and Tony's young son John to visit her relatives in Wales. A watchful Jennifer hovered all evening, swooping at the end of the night to offer Libby a bed at Home Farm rather than risk her brother compromising himself. As the days rolled on, Jennifer continued to torture herself about what, if anything, she should tell Pat, but Libby solved the problem by helpfully phoning a bemused Pat to explain she'd tidied up at Willow Farm, and hoped things were in the right place. But had her housekeeping extended to warming Tony's sheets? Not with his mother Peggy also keeping a watchful eye, so when Pat got back, Tony was genuinely able to give his wife the explanation that he'd simply felt sorry for Libby, who'd recently broken off her engagement. But Pat knew the score. She firmly told Tony she wasn't about to let him out of her sight again, though if she'd known that Libby's fantasy man was the actor Robert Redford, she might have been rather less concerned about Libby's designs on her somewhat less than Hollywood-heartthrob husband.

TONY ARCHER AND SANDY

'Farmer seeks girlfriend with own tractor. Please send photograph… of tractor'. So runs the whiskery joke about the personal ad once placed in a farming paper – but for Tony Archer, it rang all too true. Pat realised she had a rival for Tony's affections when he went out to buy a refrigerated van and came back with a rusty old Ferguson TE20 ('A classic, Pat – and only £250 – a bargain!') but when Sandy, a girl on the same course at agricultural college as their nineteen-year-old son John, started taking an interest as well, Pat and Tony's relationship sputtered to a grinding halt. Over the summer of 1995, Tony and Sandy tinkered for hours as he lovingly accumulated all the spare parts and equipment for the restoration – paint, tyres, a special Ferguson jack and a spanner from Phil, not to mention a water pump from Sandy's machinery dealer father. Seemingly oblivious to Pat's fury as her pasteuriser went unwired and the cold store unpainted, Tony lavished as much care and attention on the little grey tractor as, it seemed, Sandy was lavishing on him. After a stranded Sandy spent a night in the Bridge Farm caravan, Pat accused Tony of spending it there with her, after which he moved into it anyway in pique. In the end their marriage was cranked back into life when Sandy found herself a boyfriend with a passion for old motorbikes. Had she always truly been more interested in the machine than the man?

PAT ARCHER AND ROGER COOMBES

Did they or didn't they? There's no doubt that throughout 1984 Pat would have liked to with Roger Coombes, the lecturer on her Women's Studies course at Borchester Tech. Even the usually myopic Tony could see that Pat had been showing signs of restlessness for months, cancelling his beloved *Daily Express* in favour of *The Guardian*, for heaven's sake, and taking the children with her on a peace march. But when he challenged her about his rival on a rare family day out at the seaside, she played the innocent:

TONY	Is he after you?
PAT	Oh, I'm such a good catch aren't I, middle-aged mother of three?
TONY	Maybe he's not much of a catch either. And you're not middle-aged.
PAT	I'm getting that way. He's interesting, and good company –
TONY	And I suppose I'm not either of those things.
PAT	I'm not comparing you with Roger. I'm just saying… he's a friend of mine.
TONY	Just a friend?
PAT	(FIRM) Yes, a friend. Oh no, Tommy's making for the sea again. (GETS UP, GOING) It's all right, I'll fetch him…

Exit, pursued by a guilty conscience? By the autumn Shula and Jill, regular babysitters, were noting that three-year-old Tommy was clingy and none of the children very happy, while Pat and Tony were the picture of misery. With Pat's trysts with Roger in local pubs becoming glaringly obvious, vicar Richard Adamson had a quiet word with her, but it was Tony himself who turned things round, taking himself off to a conference and coming back with the ground-breaking news that he wanted to turn Bridge Farm organic. This ticked all the right boxes for Pat and she committed wholeheartedly once again to the farm and her marriage. Her relationship with Roger had to go: it would obviously not have gained Soil Association approval.

PEGGY WOOLLEY AND CONN KORTCHMAR

Somewhere in the loft at The Lodge, there's a faded Chinese fan. Peggy Woolley (then Peggy Perkins, later Peggy Archer) won it with her GI sweetheart, Conn, on their first date in the early 1940s at the American Red Cross Club. It was the spot prize for the couple with the best jitterbug. Peggy might have thought that was all in the past, but when Conn, now widowed, arrived in Ambridge in August 1992, as the result of mischievous prank by her granddaughter Kate, Peggy, newly married to Jack, seemed only too happy to relive her lost youth. Conn was over in England to see his son, who lived in Bristol, but family responsibilities didn't take up all his time. Jack sulked while Conn and Peggy reminisced about dance marathons in the Samson and Hercules ballroom, not to mention Conn whirling Peggy off to Borchester tea dances. As so often, it took wise words from Jill to put Jack straight: she knew that as time wore on, Peggy was in fact finding Conn a little overwhelming, and between them they managed to deflect him onto an all-too-willing Marjorie Antrobus. Ever the charmer, Conn deftly managed to juggle both women until he said his farewells on Bonfire Night. He told Peggy she'd always be his 'Peg O'My Heart' and presented her with his Zippo lighter, with which, along with so many other US servicemen, he'd burnt his name into the ceiling of a pub in Cambridge. To Marjorie, he promised that it was 'Au revoir, not adieu' and, when she still appeared disconsolate, reassured her: 'Way to go, Marjorie, way to go.'

In a couple of poignant codas, Conn's visit prompted Marjorie to organise a Wartime Revue for the village that Christmas, while Peggy contacted Conn again in 2010. Jack was by this time suffering from Alzheimer's and living at The Laurels and milkman Harry Mason helped Peggy to get in touch with her former boyfriend over the internet. Conn, Peggy learnt, had moved to a retirement community in Florida, where he could enjoy eight different golf courses and fifteen recreation centres – and, no doubt, the attentions of a posse of possible Mrs Conn Kortchmars.

PEGGY WOOLLEY AND TED GRIFFITHS

Ted's wife, Violet, is a fellow Alzheimer's sufferer and resident at The Laurels, where Peggy's husband Jack is now cared for. After nearly getting her fingers burnt with Conn – or at least by his Zippo lighter – Peggy was circumspect to say the least when Ted started making friendly overtures and suggesting cups of coffee and sandwich lunches. But when an appalled Peggy found her husband and his wife holding hands, Ted was able to explain sensitively that neither Jack nor Violet knew what they were doing, so she shouldn't take it too much to heart. This was a breakthrough in their relationship. Peggy agreed to have lunch with Ted and to go to a lecture on Richard Dadd which he was giving at the University of the Third Age. Ex-art teacher Ted also turned out to be a dab hand at enamelling, a skill he passed on to both Peggy and Jill, who as a result went head to head with their enamelled brooches at the 2011 Flower and Produce Show.

NEIL CARTER AND MAUREEN TRAVIS

'Call me Mo – all my friends do…' she smiled. Red alert! Though sadly not to the ever-trusting Neil Carter, then an animal feed rep, and calling at Hill Farm in the hope of securing an order from Maureen's husband, Geoff. But with Geoff often out of the way long-distance lorry-driving for extra cash and her daughter Becky in the same class as Neil and Susan's daughter Emma, lonely 'Mo' lost no time in cosying up to the entire Carter family. If Susan hadn't been distracted by her wayward brother Clive Horrobin absconding from custody and demanding her help to evade recapture, she might have seen through Mo, but Clive was re-arrested and swore to Susan: 'I'll take you down with me.' She was duly sentenced to six months for perverting the course of justice, and Mo seized her moment. Still in shock from Susan's imprisonment, Neil rashly agreed to bring Emma and Christopher over to Hill Farm for a sleepover, little suspecting that his sleepover was to be with Mo. His 'No, Mo!' as she attempted to seduce him rattled the plates on the dresser, but not as much as when Susan, on release, found out about her so-called friend's treachery and, possibly having picked up some bad habits inside, called round, told her what for, and gave her an almighty shove.

PHIL ARCHER AND ZOE FREEMAN

Brookfield's suffered outbreaks of several diseases over the years – foot-and-mouth, TB, spontaneous abortion – but nymphomania was one that Phil Archer was definitely unprepared for in 1972 when Jill, in need of a break after the strain of five-year-old Elizabeth's second heart operation, took herself off to visit an old school friend in London, leaving Phil with the children. Zoe Freeman was a troubled woman in an unhappy marriage to a botanist, Robin, who was warden of the then Field Centre at Arkwright Hall and, over the weeks that Jill was away, Zoe manufactured numerous flimsy excuses to drop round to Brookfield…

ZOE	I brought you a flask of coffee...
PHIL	Did... er, did you?
ZOE	Here. (FLASK)
PHIL	Thanks. That's very nice of you – but you shouldn't really.
ZOE	It's such a cold morning. I thought you might be glad of it.
PHIL	Oh, I am. It's very welcome.
ZOE	And I put a tiny – just a drop – of rum in it.
PHIL	Hey, you'll have me thinking it's my birthday.
ZOE	I'm sure that's what Jill did every morning when you were living together... I mean, when she was at home.
PHIL	Yes... oh yes. Yes she did... (POURING) I'll let you have the flask back...
ZOE	No need to guzzle it, Phil... I'll call round for it later.

Aargh! A more worldly-wise man might have seen the approaching danger, or a more opportunistic one, what was on offer, but Phil, apparently did not. (Or did he? If so he took his secret to the grave.) But that evening, as promised, Zoe turned up at Brookfield.

PHIL	I've washed the flask out.
ZOE	Never mind that, Phil.
PHIL	I'll just get it.
ZOE	Phil.
PHIL	Yes.
ZOE	Robin's away tonight. Gone to a conference in Buxton somewhere in the frozen north.
PHIL	Should be interesting.
ZOE	Very interesting.... And I thought me being on my own and you being on your own, we could drive down to the Coach House Club. A meal? A few drinks?
PHIL	Sounds tempting, but –
ZOE	Let me tempt you even further. How long is it since a woman put her arms round you – like this? And kissed you – like this? (KISS. DOOR OPENS)
PHIL	Shula!!
SHULA	I'm sorry – !

Zoe, the minx, promptly told Phil's father, Dan, that Phil had tried to kiss her – and that she'd be telling her husband about it on his return. When Dan challenged Phil, Phil explained the circumstances but, ever the gentleman, felt the blame should reside with him: if he hadn't exactly led Zoe on, then at least he must have somehow given her the wrong impression. It had all been his fault. And that, he told his dad, was what he'd tell Robin when he got back from his conference. Dan wasn't having that and, indignant about his son's innocence, tried to intercede on Phil's behalf. Robin, however, seemed unwilling to listen.

DAN	I've had a talk with my son.
ROBIN	And I've had a talk with my wife.
DAN	But I'd like you to hear –
ROBIN	Mr Archer, I've a tremendous respect for you. But what I've got to say is for Philip's ears – and his alone.
DAN	But you've got to hear both sides.
ROBIN	I don't need to hear both sides.
DAN	It isn't like you to be biased.
ROBIN	But I am, Mr Archer. Very biased.

When Phil and Robin finally met, everything seemed set for a showdown:

ROBIN	Zoe told me you put your arms around her, and tried to kiss her.
PHIL	I'm sorry, Robin. I don't know what came over me.
ROBIN	You don't deny it then?
PHIL	It… it just seemed to happen. I'd not planned it, if that's what you think.
ROBIN	Do you really want to know what I think?

PHIL	What?
ROBIN	That you're a liar.
PHIL	Robin, believe me. The thought hadn't entered my head. It just happened. I'm sorry.
ROBIN	Zoe kissed *you*.
PHIL	Is that what she said?
ROBIN	No.
PHIL	Then you're not taking her word?
ROBIN	I wish I could. But you're not the first, Phil. And you'll not be the last.
PHIL	Oh!
ROBIN	Her hobby is... men. It's a weakness, like being an alcoholic. She can't help herself.

After all that.... In the meantime, fourteen-year-old Shula had told Jill what she'd seen, and Phil shot to London to reassure his wife and explain about Zoe's psychological problems. Jill understood, and in due course came home. But the traumatic experience for poor Shula, who only came in to ask her father a question about her homework, is something she's never talked about...

PHIL ARCHER AND MYRA

If the Borsetshire criminal fraternity trembled when they came up before local magistrate Myra in the late 1970s and early 1980s, so too did fellow JP Phil Archer when he knew he'd be sitting alongside her on the Bench. Back in the Brookfield kitchen, his breathless accounts of her fearless sentencing meant that his amused children soon detected something of a crush and eyebrows were raised when Phil and Myra departed together for a two-day magistrates' conference. Phil always stoutly maintained that any feelings towards Myra amounted to nothing more than admiration for her professional capabilities, but that may simply be the confidentiality of the court....

PHIL ARCHER AND HEATHER PRITCHARD

When Ruth's mother, Heather Pritchard, came to stay at Brookfield in 2003, she discovered that she and Phil had a shared passion – for musicals. Soon they were enjoying, if not enchanted evenings, then musical afternoons, and trotting off to concerts together. When married to Solly, Heather had never impinged on Phil and Jill's relationship, but, newly widowed, could she really pose a serious threat to Ambridge's lodestar couple? Heather's gentle prattle about Phil being the perfect 'date' ('He treated me to a programme and explained all about the arias!') didn't go down at all well with Jill and when both grannies turned up to collect the children from the school bus, Jill, who'd abandoned the church flowers half-done to be there, suggested coolly that Ruth draw up a rota. There were more tests for Jill's blood pressure when she discovered that Phil had swanned off to the library on a quest for Rodgers and Hammerstein CDs, and when he forgot to mend Jill's hen coop in favour of showing fascinated Heather his veg plot. But things really came to the boil when Heather challenged Jill on her home territory, the kitchen, by making some marmalade. Over the Glebe Cottage breakfast table, it turned into a sticky situation:

JILL	This isn't my marmalade.
PHIL	No, it's Heather's.
JILL	(DELIBERATELTY LIGHT) Heather's.
PHIL	She brought a jar down the other day.
JILL	I see.
PHIL	She's made a load of it for Brookfield, apparently.
JILL	Has she?
PHIL	I just shoved it at the back of the cupboard but I thought we'd better try it to show willing.
JILL	Of course...
PHIL	I had some myself. I thought it was quite nice...

Jill kept her own counsel. But at breakfast a few days later Phil seemed to have come, at last, to his senses.

JILL	(SITS) Oh! Two sorts of marmalade...
PHIL	Yes. Yours and Heather's.
JILL	(BEAT. CAREFUL) I think I'll have honey this morning.
PHIL	Right... (JAR) And I'm going to have some of this.
JILL	(EVER SO SLIGHT NOTE OF TRIUMPH) Mine.
PHIL	(LID OFF JAR) Yes. I think I find Heather's a bit... sickly.

There would be no oven gloves at dawn. The marmalade wars were over.

THEY LOVED AND LOST

DAVID AND RUTH

At first glance, David and Ruth have one of those Teflon-coated marriages, to which nothing mucky will stick. Yet the edifice came close to tumbling down when David spent too much time with his ex and Ruth sought solace in the arms of a cowman. Together they proved that two wrongs do not make anything right.

Back in 1986, David had proposed to posh Sophie Barlow as they watched the Royal Wedding of Prince Andrew and Sarah Ferguson together. A half-hearted courtship finally fizzled out after Sophie moved to London and David became ensconced on the farm.

Fast forward 20 years and David was astounded to see his glamorous, fashion designer ex at a local fundraiser. Indeed, everyone in the family was delighted to see her back in Ambridge, with the notable exception of Ruth. As David threw himself into fundraising with Sophie – and out of family life – Ruth got more disgruntled. And by the time he realised he risked losing everything for Sophie's playful amusement, Ruth had already found comfort with the accommodating Sam.

It was only a matter of time before the illicit pair plotted a night away together, free from David's gaze. The marriage was failing but David, still blissfully ignorant about the assignation, was still confident it would survive when Pip asked: 'Is she coming back?'

PIP	Dad, I can see what things are like. I'm not stupid.
DAVID	I know you're not. Look sweetheart, I'm not going to pretend. OK, me and Mum haven't been getting on that well lately –
PIP	Understatement of several centuries.
DAVID	But we're sorting it out, you know. It just takes time, that's all.
PIP	And part of sorting it out is her going away?
DAVID	Well, yeah. All couples need a break from one another now and again.

But between Brookfield Farm and the hotel they had booked in Oxford there was rush-hour traffic that condemned Ruth to hours spent brooding in a car on a marriage of largely happy memories.

A timely telephone message from Pip ultimately brought forth sufficient sickening guilt to prevent Ruth from consummating her relationship with Sam. As the champagne awaiting her warmed to room temperature, the bubble burst for them both.

RUTH	I'm sorry. I'm really sorry.
SAM	Just come inside.
RUTH	No.
SAM	Please. At least we can talk properly there.
RUTH	I can't, Sam. I can't.
SAM	But – you've come all this way.

RUTH	I know.
SAM	What's changed? What's changed your mind?
RUTH	Everything. Everything.
SAM	Look, you've had a horrible journey. You're tired –
RUTH	It's not that. Please, Sam, I can't do it.
SAM	But –
RUTH	I can't do it to David – to the kids – deceiving him and them. The lies I've told. I've lied to him more in the last two weeks than in the last 18 years.
SAM	I know you hate lying.
RUTH	I can't do it. I can't do it any more.
SAM	But what about me? You love me.
RUTH	I'm sorry.
SAM	You love me, don't you?
RUTH	Yes, you know I do. I do love you and I know you love me but I can't be with you.
SAM	No.
RUTH	I mean it. I'm sorry but I can't do it. I can't go through with this. I can't go through with any of it. Oh Sam, I'm so sorry.

She returned home, a changed woman. But after she admitted to being in love with Sam, David became cold and angry. A tree house largely built by Sam in the absence of the flirtatious David was hacked into matchwood in a frustrated form of revenge.

For months the marriage staggered on, kept alive only by work and the needs of the children. Close friends Usha and Alan tried to mediate, pointing out that the mild romances really cancelled one another out. After all, neither affair had amounted to anything naughtier than a kiss. Finally Ruth and David made up, shaken by the frailties of human nature and chastened by their dangerous liaisons.

PAUL AND LILIAN

Paul was the surprise addition to Matt's family who arrived on the scene in 2010. Their mother was dying, and Paul was hoping for some fraternal support, despite a lifetime spent apart. On the downside, he discovered Matt was in prison. On the upside, he found Lilian, whose nerves had been raked by Matt's sentence and whose confidence was at a low ebb following Matt's coldness. Both were tempted by the thought of a relationship but it stayed a chaste affair in those early days. Only when they reconnected two years later was the passion unleashed. When this fully fledged affair came to an abrupt end, there would be no going back. In the days of innocence, here's how the love birds parted prior to Matt's return from prison:

PAUL — No, listen to me. You're a wonderful woman, Lilian. You're warm, witty, great company... You're lovely. And so attractive... I've fallen in love with you, deeply in love with you. And I can't stand the thought of losing you now. And I know you have feelings for me, too. I can tell when we're together... You do, don't you?

LILIAN (BEAT) Yes.

PAUL I realised it properly for the first time only recently. I knew I was falling for you, but I wasn't thinking, wasn't focusing on it. I don't know if it was because I didn't dare to, or maybe... *(was scared to...)*

LILIAN (QUIETLY) Yes.

PAUL I don't want you to be with Matt. I want you to be with me. Is there any chance that you feel even a little bit the same? That your feelings for Matt might have changed? (LONG PAUSE)

LILIAN Oh, Paul, you make me feel so good. You make me feel wanted. Needed. Desired. And you're such a wonderful man, Paul. Strong and loving and warm... And so open and generous... I do have feelings for you –

PAUL Lilian – ! (HE MOVES TO TAKE HER IN HIS ARMS BUT SHE STEPS AWAY)

LILIAN No!

PAUL But – ?

LILIAN	I'm sorry. I've loved every minute of your company, Paul, and your friendship has meant so much. I am very, very fond of you. I can't help it – you're a wonderful man. But Matt and I have been together a long time. It might sound like a cliché, but we've been through a lot together, good times and bad. And I've supported him and stood by him...
PAUL	I see.
LILIAN	My future life is with him.
PAUL	(BIG SIGH)
LILIAN	(BEAT THEN A SMALL HOPE) We can still see each other. It would be lovely if the three of us could be friends? (A GULF OPENS BETWEEN THEM – THEY BOTH KNOW IT'S NEVER GOING TO HAPPEN)
PAUL	Yes, maybe...
LILIAN	After all we are practically family...
PAUL	True.
LILIAN	But I can't promise any more than that, Paul. I'm so sorry.
PAUL	Not as sorry as I am. But you do understand – I had to ask?
LILIAN	Yes.

PAUL — Just in case the miracle happened... and you said 'yes'. I couldn't let the loveliest woman I've ever met go, without her knowing how I felt. (PAUSE) I should go.

LILIAN — Oh wait! (SHE HUGS HIM. AND THEY BOTH CLING ON FOR A SECOND TOO LONG, KNOWING IT'S THE LAST TIME. PAUL BREAKS AWAY)

PAUL — Bye, Lilian. Good luck. I wish you all the happiness in the world. (<u>HE WALKS AWAY AND GENTLY SHUTS THE DOOR BEHIND HIM. LILIAN CLUTCHES THE BACK OF A CHAIR AND CHOKES BACK A SOB</u>.) (<u>MUSIC</u>)

VILLAGE LIFE

URBAN DWELLERS VIEW VILLAGE life with envy, believing there to be crime-free streets, cheery residents and apple-cheeked children with smiles on their faces and songs in their hearts. Such universal conviviality is rarely found. Villagers, like city folk, find their lives marked by crime, crisis and calamities as well as a host of niggles and quirks. In Ambridge, neighbours – who are good friends – fall out with alarming regularity over issues great and small.

Sometimes neighbours turn out to be arch villains who must be brought to book by judge and jury. Conspiracies of misfortune and bad timing bring others to the dock. However, it tends to be more low-key events that evoke the strongest feelings. Take the Flower and Produce Show, for example. A tremendous will to win (the prize being a rosette or similar) drives some competitors to extraordinary lengths. Prize vegetables and baking are inevitably the most hard-fought categories.

Indeed, food remains at the heart of village life, varying from gastronomic delicacy to home-cooked delight. There are badly kept secrets in a village, and well-masked wisdom that will out on rare occasions. In Ambridge, life is sufficiently green and pleasant to attract celebrities who cause more ripples of excitement than a stone thrown in the village pond.

EVERYBODY NEEDS GOOD NEIGHBOURS

The art of the verbal sideswipe is frequently honed in Ambridge. Rapier words that would leave most regular victims reeling are dispensed regularly, the smiling assassin left licking their disdainful lips. But they breed them tough in Borsetshire and the average Ambridgite won't notice a scathing tone or cloaked insult. Or if they do register, the impact on the Richter scale is a big, fat zero.

This was certainly Clarrie's response when Lynda Snell made some waspish comments as she put up new and fashionably busy wallpaper at Grange Farm:

CLARRIE	Are there any big bubbles?
LYNDA	There are so many patterns on that paper, Clarrie, I doubt if I'd notice a hot air balloon, let alone a bubble.
CLARRIE	Cheerful though, don't you think?
LYNDA	Positively manic, almost verging on the frenzied.
CLARRIE	We can't all have the same taste.
LYNDA	No, quite.

CLARRIE	It's the latest style this, you know. Two different patterns, top and bottom. What it really needs is a fancy border.
LYNDA	I suppose if you added yet another pattern it might all cancel itself out.

In 1993, an outraged Robert complained to Brian about noxious smoke created by burning crop stubble.

ROBERT	But you've left the whole corner of one field.
BRIAN	Two or three acres, that's not worth the trouble.
ROBERT	You are going to burn that too?
BRIAN	It's only worth about seventy quid an acre.
ROBERT	Oh really, so why bother to grow it?
BRIAN	Because I get a pretty decent area subsidy just for planting the stuff, what I make on the crop is just a bonus.
ROBERT	This is just incredible. I can't believe I'm hearing this.

BRIAN	I'm just telling you the facts.
ROBERT	You farmers – you just don't know you're born.

Brian wasn't impressed when an elderly Uncle Tom, staying at Home Farm in 1993 after his wife Pru needed full-time care, made one reminiscence too many after suffering the perceived indignity of a cold bath.

TOM	Before we had a bathroom, my Pru used to fill the tin bath every Friday night with water she boiled up in pans.
BRIAN	(QUIETLY) No wonder she's in a home.

In the early 1970s, pub landlady Polly Perks and barmaid Nora McAuley, who considered herself a cut above, were trying out some crisps in the daring, newly launched prawn cocktail flavour when Polly had a rare chance for a putdown:

NORA	You can't taste the prawns.
POLLY	Well, it says on the packet they are for the discerning palate.

There was a slightly more loving rejoinder from Laura Archer, Dan's sister-in-law who arrived from New Zealand in 1957 with deep pockets and a big heart, to Colonel Freddie Danby in 1980 when she happened across his prone figure at their home, Ambridge Hall.

DANBY	Oh I wasn't asleep m'dear. Not a bit of it.
LAURA	Oh no?
DANBY	Meditating m'dear – eyes closed, brain in neutral, drawing on the mystic forces of the mind you know. Recharging the old batteries.
LAURA	And snoring at the same time?

In 1999, a famously disconsolate Kate Aldridge was working in the village shop, brooding on her bad luck to be stuck inside on a Sunday at what felt like the back end of the universe. She was lucky to have a job, mum Jennifer pointed out, inadvertently offering Kate the chance to take a pop at everyone in the community:

> Yeah, it's a job. In Ambridge – bustling, cosmopolitan, once seen, never forgotten Ambridge. I should count myself lucky really. I'd hate to be stuck somewhere dull.

Years later she had her comeuppance from no less a figure than grandmother Peggy when Kate – who has spent much of her time on a different continent to daughter Phoebe – claimed maternal rights during a harvest supper:

PEGGY	May I remind you Roy and Haley have the day to day authority over Phoebe. And it's very confusing for the child when you undermine them like this.
KATE	That may be true Gran –
PEGGY	It is.
KATE	– and I don't want to argue... but Phoebe is *my* daughter. *I* gave birth to her, and I'm her real mother.
PEGGY	(BEAT. CUTTING) Only when it suits you, dear.

BY ANY OTHER NAME

Has there ever been a good egg in Ambridge called Simon? With the sole exception of Simon Cooper, the trusty farmhand at Brookfield in the 1950s, and possibly Caroline's brother Simon, about whom nothing is known but his name, every Simon who's set foot in the village has been a bad lot.

First there was *Borchester Echo* reporter Simon Parker. When Shula was looking for a job following her stint at secretarial college, he splashed a story about her entitled 'Hunting on the Dole', was unaccountably forgiven, made love to her in a cornfield, then unceremoniously dumped her when he got a job offer in London.

When Shula finally did secure a job at local estate agent Rodway and Watson's, she immediately ran into another Simon. The uncompromising Simon Trent claimed to be fair when valuing items for distress sales or evaluating dilapidations at the end of a tenancy but operated, according to one local farmer, by 'fancy handshakes in the car park at the back of The Feathers after a five-course lunch at his customers' expense'. Beware…

Then came Simon Gerrard – one of Debbie's lecturers at University. After a failed affair with him in which he'd been two-timing her, Debbie came home to lick her wounds. But he sought her out and charmed both her and, inevitably, Jennifer – he was a Professor of Literature, after all. Brian was never taken in, worrying that Simon was after Debbie's inheritance, but also worrying about patterns of behaviour (it takes one to know one). Sure enough, having secured at job at Felpersham University, Simon was soon accused of sexual harassment by a student, but managed to slime his way out of it. Debbie forgave him but when, some months later, his mobile phone bill revealed a succession of calls to the same number, his affair with a woman called Jeanette was exposed and their marriage was over.

Not learning from their experiences, in the late 1990s Shula and Debbie each took another man called Simon into their lives. Simon Pemberton was the son of Caroline's first husband Guy, who was the owner of the Estate. Mixed-up and volatile, Simon was violent, first to Shula, and then to Debbie, who bravely gave evidence against him in a subsequent court case. There's currently a vacancy in Ambridge… for a Saintly Simon.

FARM YARN

Lean at the farm gate with an old-timer like Jethro and you might expect a meandering story or two. Trouble is, can you be sure he's telling the truth? When he recounted the following saga about a man with a deaf horse, his audience was split 50/50. Dan Archer called him an old leg puller, but Dan's daughter-in-law Jill was intrigued.

JETHRO	Plough horse it was… and it gradually became one of the sights of the neighbourhood, you know, this 'ere deaf horse.
JILL	What did it do?

JETHRO	This 'ere stop-start lark.
DAN	Oh get on with it, Jethro, and let's get some work done.
JILL	Where does the stop-start thing come in, Jethro?
JETHRO	I be just a-telling ya! Didn't matter what it was doing: pulling the plough or a Narrer or a drill or anything. It'd just tek two or three paces ferrard and then stop and listen.
DAN	Oh pull the other one.
JETHRO	It's the truth... Cos he was deaf y'see, poor old critter.
JILL	But what was it listening for?
JETHRO	It was listening to see if the farmer was shouting 'Whoa'. You see, it couldn't hear while it was pulling the implement y'see, cos o'the noise.

APRIL FOOLERY

Ambridge residents have sometimes observed the niceties of April Fool's Day, playing elaborate hoaxes with a sense of decorum. On other occasions it is an excuse to settle old scores.

Elizabeth failed to see the funny side when her former boyfriend Tim Beecham sprayed 'Elizabeth Archer wears thermal vests' on a wall opposite Borchester magistrates' court in 1986. So did Phil, who promptly banned him from Brookfield. So did the magistrates, who fined him £200 and ordered him to pay £200 compensation. The mood was not improved by Jethro's dog Gyp, when he pulled the vest in question from the rubbish and dragged it around the farmyard.

In 1992, the joke was on Eddie when he was caught frantically metal detecting in St Stephen's churchyard, having heard from Debbie that sovereigns looted from Netherbourne Hall were almost certainly nestling among the gravestones. Fool's gold indeed. Only a gentle reminder by the vicar about the date sent Eddie back home, with his tail between his legs.

It was Eddie's turn to pull a prank in 1999, though, as he persuaded Joe they must photograph all the cows for their soon-to-be-mandatory animal passports. Joe spent a muddy morning trying to get each member of his herd to look into the camera before clocking the date.

Two years later, young Ed fell back on that hardy chestnut, the coin superglued to the ground, to get his April Fool's Day kicks. Moreover he hid in a bush with a camera to catch people aimlessly scratching at the ground.

At Brookfield, the best and oft-repeated joke is to present family members with empty boiled eggs, an art refined by Ruth's dad, Solly Pritchard.

Indeed, all the most successful jokes involve an element of preparation. Pat and Tony plotted long and hard over lunch on how to bring Lilian to book after she had casually caused offence. Their creative thinking was fuelled by the contents of a wine bottle. On the big day, Lilian got a letter trumpeting the powers of a new facial product called Lipo Flora and she embarked on a search of Borsetshire for it. It was days later in the pub before her credulity – not realising Lipo Flora was an anagram of April Fool – came to light.

When Eddie was told he must take part in a local town crier's competition speaking Italian he practised hard and gave it a go. Little did he suspect as he bellowed out at his operatic best that Bert, Freda and Jolene had faked the instructions ostensibly sent to him by the organisers. Bert added value to the joke by insisting he was going to do his entry in Swedish.

Pip showed she had the full measure of her parents when, aged almost 15, she texted them following a sleepover, asking for a lift from a boy's house. Both were in meltdown when they received a further text, moments later, claiming they were 'April Fools'.

Kenton was cock-a-hoop with his tattoo which, as far as he was concerned, was the ornate Cantonese characters for 'Lucky in every endeavour'. Kathy, his partner in 2009, seized a calendar opportunity to cut him down to size, in cahoots with pal Lorna. Claiming she could read Cantonese, Lorna insisted the tattoo meant 'closed for cleaning' and Kenton was duly distraught. Only eventually did they come clean themselves.

Lynda was the target of Jim's intellectual jape when he told her Ovid's *Metamorphoses* was the next choice for the book club. But it was literary warrior Richard Thwaite who came off worst as he gamely began reading the opus.

TABLE TALK

No one enjoyed his food more than gamekeeper Tom Forrest, Doris Archer's brother, 'Uncle Tom' to the Archer family but 'Fatman Forrest' to the less respectful Eddie Grundy. On a typical Sunday evening at Keeper's Cottage in the 1970s, the fat was chewed, literally:

TOM	(CARVING COLD MEAT) Fancy a bit of both?
PRU	Yes please. Marry it up.
TOM	I reckon half the flavour's in the fat.
PRU	There's been a lot of talk about animal fat not being good for you.
TOM	Ar, talk, and most folks have got it wrong, as usual.
PRU	Chutney or pickles?
TOM	Bit of both, please.
PRU	You'll never be slim and willowy.
TOM	Don't want to be. Bert Gibbs called me 'The Great Mr Forrest' the other day. Referring to my bay window.

PRU	Oh him! Nobody wants to take any notice of him.
TOM	A lot do. He's clever, too, in an okkerd kind of a way.
PRU	He reads the papers, I know. And listens to the wireless a lot. But all the same...!

Another Ambridge intellectual skewered in a sentence.

BACKHANDER

Pru Forrest wasn't always the meek, damson-bottling paragon she's made out to be. When Jack Woolley employed her and her husband Tom to run his garden centre, she could see through her boss with no trouble. When Jack presented The Bull's barmaid Nora McAuley with a box of petunias and salvias with his compliments, Pru wasn't taken in, sniffing that it was 'a Brummagem gift', meaning 'you can have it; I don't want it.' It was, she pointed out, rather late in the year for bedding plants, and Woolley was right to conclude that Nora might as well have them. They'd only be sold off for next to nothing – or even thrown away.

I FOUGHT THE LAW

At first glance, villages like Ambridge appear to have peaceful streets inhabited by law-abiding and upright citizens. But its sixty-year history tells a different story…

ANGEL GABRIEL?

In 1967, Walter Gabriel's son Nelson initially bore all the hallmarks of being a wrong 'un. Poor Walter was grief-stricken and alone at the airport when he believed his son was dead in a plane crash. Only later did he discover that Nelson had no intention of getting the flight and had faked his own death. Soon afterwards he was arrested by police for a mail-van robbery, charges Nelson branded as 'idiotic' and 'tedious'. Throughout the ordeal, Walter's enduring support in public for his only son was tempered by privately held doubts. Villagers rallied around him without necessarily expressing support for Nelson.

NELSON That's the way they are playing it, is it? Offering their heartfelt sympathy to a poor old man whose only son turned out to be a ne'er-do-well.

WALTER Mmm, am you a ne'er-do-well, Nelson?

NELSON	What I am or what I'm not is entirely beside the point. I'm quite sure the Ambridge-ites – does one say Ambridge-ites by the way or Ambridgians?
WALTER	I never says neither personally.
NELSON	Well, as I was saying, I'm quite sure the Ambridgites have blackened my character to the utmost limits.
WALTER	They 'em not a lot of unfeeling thick heads you know, Nelson. They 'em honest, decent, hardworking...
NELSON	Yes? Go on, say it, my most unfavourite word.
WALTER	Respectable.
NELSON	That's it, that's the one.

Eventually, Nelson was freed after a jury found him not guilty in a majority verdict after Walter inadvertently laid a false trail in a Sunday newspaper interview he'd given. 'I was proud of you, you didn't put a foot wrong. You made a splendid smoke screen,' Nelson told a baffled Walter.

Nelson refused to stay around despite Walter's pleadings but, Terminator-style, warned: 'My dear aged parent, I'll be back, have no fear.'

LOVE AND DEATH

Tom Forrest was the last person anyone expected to see in the dock. But in 1957 that's just where he found himself, charged with manslaughter.

The victim was Bob Larkin, who died after Tom and Phil staked out the Fairbrother estate in the night time to nab poachers. There was a struggle in the darkness and Bob's body fell limp and lifeless to the floor. Tom's gun had gone off and Bob had been shot in the head.

The case was complicated because Tom had been heard making threats to Bob Larkin; both men had an interest in barmaid Pru Harris, and when Bob got too familiar with her, Tom felt the need to warn him off.

After his arrest, Tom, a man used to wide open spaces, was imprisoned for a while before being remanded on bail. Fortunately, a jury was swift in dismissing the charges. Tom returned to Ambridge to the triumphant sounds of the Hollerton silver band and into the arms of the waiting Pru.

CLIVE HORROBIN AND THE REVOLVING PRISON DOOR

The amiable and meandering conversations of the village shop were cut short on a spring day in 1993 when two masked men burst in wielding a gun, demanding cash and cigarettes.

Betty was serving Jack Woolley at the time while Kate and sister Debbie got caught up in the drama after Kate let down the getaway van's tyres. And no one cared about the few hundred pounds taken after Jack collapsed with heart problems provoked by the stress. Within a few days Clive Horrobin had been arrested and charged. He was a local lad and brother of Susan Carter. It was the next step in a criminal career that took him through a revolving prison door.

Clive escaped from custody and Susan found herself embroiled in a subterfuge that also led to a prison cell. Without telling husband Neil – or the police – she provided money for the fugitive and helped him dye his hair. She even agreed to take his passport and some clothes to Birmingham. But when his plan to flee was foiled, he implicated her to the police and she too was arrested.

Shortly before Christmas she stood in the dock beside her errant brother to hear him sentenced to seven years and to receive a six-month sentence herself for attempting to pervert the course of justice. She compounded her problems by absconding herself a couple of months later to attend the funeral of Mark Hebden, Shula's husband and the solicitor who had done so much to help her.

By 1997, Clive was out of jail and consumed with the desire for vengeance against George Barford who, by convoluted logic, he decided was to blame for his poor lot in life. There followed a raid on The Stables, where the Barfords were living, and a vicious assault on George himself, for which Eddie Grundy was firmly in the frame. Finally, Clive was nailed and dispatched back to prison for five years.

It wasn't the last Ambridge had heard of the unprepossessing Clive. In 2003, there was a series of nasty horse slashings at The Stables, by now run by Shula and Alistair. Terrified by these sinister events, they had no idea why they were being targeted. When Clive was proven to be the perpetrator it became apparent he believed the Barfords still lived there. When he discovered his mistake, Clive didn't express remorse, rather satisfaction that the Barfords' niece, Shula, had been distressed.

After receiving the maximum sentence of four months, Clive was back – and this time he meant business. One of his first acts after being freed was to hold George and Christine Barford at gunpoint in their home, the Old Police House. When Phil called unexpectedly Clive made his escape with shotgun still in hand.

Little more than a week later, Clive returned to petrol bomb the home, leaving Christine and Jill trapped inside. Lucky for them David, who was drinking at The Bull, smashed a window so they could escape. Clive was himself badly burned. It left Christine terrified that she was still at risk and she confided her fears to vicar Alan Franks:

CHRIS	After the horse slashing they said he'd be going down for a long time. And he didn't.
ALAN	But this time...
CHRIS	Then they said he'd never try anything again – but he did.
ALAN	I understand.
CHRIS	Then after he took us hostage they said the police would catch him.
ALAN	They've caught him now.
CHRIS	Don't you see? I was right. I was right every time.

ALAN	Yes, you were.
CHRIS	Oh, thank you.
ALAN	But that doesn't mean you're right this time.
CHRIS	Doesn't it?
ALAN	Chris, the things he's done to you are terrible. He must seem like a monster.
CHRIS	Seem?
ALAN	But he's not superhuman. In fact, he's rather pathetic.
CHRIS	Don't tell me to feel sorry for him.
ALAN	He's in Birmingham. He's very badly injured. He's in a secure hospital.

Fortunately no one died in the misguided vendetta, although George Barford's death was widely thought to have been hastened by those criminal actions, for which Clive received a twelve-year sentence.

Still, he couldn't keep away from Ambridge, despite a legal restriction that banned him from the village. He was back in 2011, with agreement from the probation service, for his mother Ivy's funeral.

The following year he returned to the area, sleeping with jailed brother Keith's partner Donna and being violent to her and sister Tracy. When they finally lured him into Ambridge on a pretext, the police were waiting, and in 2013 he received another four-year jail term.

BROCK'S REVENGE

No one could fail to sympathise with David Archer when Brookfield Farm was brought to a halt after TB was found in the herd for the third time in a decade. In 2003, just two years after the tensions generated by the foot-and-mouth crisis, David and Ruth were braced for a farming catastrophe that could bring their business once more to the brink. They had to send animals to be slaughtered if they were thought to have the disease, they couldn't buy or sell cattle and accordingly they had to find the cash for extra feed.

David was convinced that badgers – known carriers of the disease – were to blame, although it was by no means a universally held opinion. When he came home to find a badger running rampant in his feed store he took his shotgun into the yard and killed it. And it wasn't the first time David has killed a badger. He shot one in similar circumstances in 1995 without being caught.

But it turned out that badgers were unlucky for David in more ways than one. Badgers are protected by a 1992 government act and he found himself landed with the carcass of an illegally killed animal. And when he tried to dump it on a verge to make it seem like road kill, he was spotted by arch nemesis Matt Crawford.

Within days Ambridge was alive with news of how David had killed the creature. Pip, Ruth and Jill were all furious with him and, when he thought it couldn't get any worse, an RSPCA inspector came calling. A few months later he was fined £400 and ordered to pay £200 in costs by magistrates.

Land agent Graham Ryder wasted no time in taunting him outside The Bull: 'I never believed you farmers were quite as hard-up as you claimed to be. Always thought you were crying wolf… or should I say badger?'

Ryder's jibe prompted David to give an impassioned speech about the effects of TB on Brookfield, having seen three more Hereford cows go to slaughter that morning. These were the grass-fed cows that were supposed to produce the quality beef people wanted after the BSE scare, intended to guarantee the future of Brookfield Farm.

> Tuberculosis is virtually an epidemic in some parts of this country, huge numbers being slaughtered, entire bloodlines lost, but because there aren't any pyres, because it's not in the papers, most people are completely unaware… It all makes work for land agents, doesn't it? But you want to remember when you're banking your bonus cheque that you're dancing on people's graves – real people, real families, who're just about at the end of their rope.

But badgers hadn't finished with the farm yet. In 2011 there was a slurry leak at Brookfield after damage to the storage reservoir caused by the sharp claws of a badger. This time the bill came to £40,000 and it was a close-run thing as to whether the Archers continued to keep the cows at all.

COSTA LIVING

No one was particularly surprised to hear that flint-hard businessman Matt Crawford had been milking money from his business accounts. Nor was anyone saddened to know that the unscrupulous wheeler-dealer would finally get his comeuppance. Except for Lilian, so wholly in love with the crook at the time that she even countenanced living abroad in Costa Rica with him.

To everyone else they were having a holiday in Spain before undergoing the stress of a trial. But the real plan was to start a new life there so Matt could escape an inevitable jail sentence. 'We are going to make a good life out here,' he promised. She seriously considered the option of flipping to and fro between the two countries in order to maintain contact with her family.

Any lure to this plan vanished when she was reduced to having staring contests with geckoes to pass the time. She begged Matt to change his stance. But her pleas fell on deaf ears, even though she insisted he was condemning her to a life sentence.

A stiff talking to from brother-in-law Brian ('don't let him drag you down with him') persuaded her to buy two flights home that would get Matt to the courthouse in time for his scheduled hearing. At first, he would not be swayed and vowed to stay on in South America.

LILIAN	What am I supposed to do?
MATT	Exactly what you do in Ambridge. Go out to lunch.
LILIAN	Who with?

MATT Me. Or have your hair done.

LILIAN Twice a day with this humidity.

MATT (SARCASTICALLY) There you are then. That will take up some time. Look, once we've got a house, we'll make some nice friends.

LILIAN I don't want friends, Matt. I want my family.

Eventually he boarded the plane, turned up at Birmingham Crown Court and was given an eighteen-month sentence for the fraud he had perpetrated, and ordered to spend a minimum of nine months behind bars.

BROOKFIELD BURNS

If David was the villain of 'dead badger' scandal he became a victim after a gang of unscrupulous farm thieves went to work in Ambridge in 2012.

The bottle spun after Adam was attacked and badly beaten. David discovered Adam's prone figure and witnessed the escape of those responsible. Fortunately, in the months afterwards Adam made a recovery. But for David problems unfolded virtually week by week as the suspects began an orchestrated campaign of intimidation to stop him giving evidence.

It began with silent phone calls, unnerving Ruth but doing little to shake David's resolve. Then there were unseen intruders, a savaged ram and a stampede. For the Brookfield Archers, there was an eerie goldfish-bowl existence, while they were being closely watched by unknown eyes.

Surveillance cameras strategically placed around the farm did little to soothe Ruth's frayed nerves. She and Jill had serious doubts about the wisdom of David's plan to give evidence in court. Usha, Adam's partner, Ian, and David himself remained convinced he had to do the right thing.

Paralysing fear finally led Ruth to send the children to her mother and Emma, at nearby Rickyard Cottage, moved home to Susan and Neil's house. But a telephone threat – and Susan's bossy ways – made everyone head to their respective homes, united in a desire to stand firm against the hidden enemy.

In fact, the drama reached its climax long before David's day in court. A July night was lit up by flames as Brookfield's barn was set on fire. Although there was wholesale damage, no one was physically hurt. However, Emma, haunted by the what-might-have-beens, was convinced she saw her Uncle Keith running from the scene. It was her turn to make an anonymous call, and the police arrested Keith Horrobin, who eventually confessed all. He had fallen in with the vicious gang after having money troubles and he received a four-year jail term for his part in the drama. Ruth and David could sleep easy again – at least until Pip's next escapade.

FIVE THINGS TO DO BEFORE A FIRE

- Direct the Christmas revue (Peggy, when her then-home, Blossom Hill Cottage, caught fire in 1983)

- Attend a Cliff Richard concert and come home singing 'We're All Going On A Summer Holiday' (Clarrie, with Betty, Susan, Brenda and Emma, in 1996, only to find the Grange Farm outbuildings ablaze)

- Do an evening of farm chores, then watch a film with your family (*Transformers* in David and Ruth's case, before the Brookfield barn blaze in July 2012)

- Have a quiet evening in with your sister-in-law (Christine and Jill at the Old Police House in 2004, unaware that Clive Horrobin was lurking outside Christine's home as part of his misguided 'revenge' campaign against her husband, George Barford)

- Plan a celebration to mark a successful day at a sheep sale (Phil and Grace Archer, John Tregorran and Carol Grey, at Grey Gables in September 1955. But barely had they chinked glasses when Grace left to look for a dropped earring, only to discover that the stables were on fire. She ran in to save a horse, Midnight, an act which cost her her life)

And for the Fire-Setter:

- Have a bonfire (A spark from an unidentified villager's day of leaf-sweeping caused the stable fire at Grey Gables)
- Chat to the local vicar (On the night of the Old Police House fire in 2004, newly arrived vicar Alan Franks stopped to offer help to Clive Horrobin when he saw him standing at the roadside with a petrol can, thinking he was a stranded motorist)
- Attend your soon-to-be son-in-law's 'last night of freedom' drinks in a local pub (Keith Horrobin, before setting the Brookfield barn on fire)
- Suffer depression following your bankruptcy (Mike Tucker who, in 1991, was on the point of torching a barn at Jim Ascott's farm before he was stopped by Eddie Grundy)
- Suffer mental problems (Sid Perks's first wife Polly's father, Frank Mead, was the cause of several blazes in and around Ambridge in the 1960s. He was committed to the local mental hospital)

NIGEL'S ECO AGENDA

Nature lover Nigel always loved the sound of birdsong and the rustle of sun-dappled leaves. They were simple pleasures that seemed endangered in a world ready to risk its very existence for the sake of big business. After he had children, Nigel embraced the green theme at his ancestral home and business, Lower Loxley, to make his corner of the world a better place for them.

- He used lambs' wool to lag the roof space rather than fibre glass.
- Ordinary light bulbs were replaced with low-energy ones.
- Ruth and David's Hereford beef was introduced to the menu.
- Nigel sold his car and took to his bike, wearing a distinctive orange cape in the rain.
- He recorded the first signs of spring in the countryside, comparing his notes with those made by his Uncle Edmund about natural phenomena a generation previously.

- Pioneering green weddings, he offered horse-drawn transport, wine made from Lower Loxley grapes, and used bird seed rather than confetti.

GOURMET GIRLS

It was February 2012. The fuss about the e-coli outbreak had finally subsided and the Bridge Farm Archers, after endless soul-searching and no little argument, had re-launched their products under the 'Ambridge Organics' label. But the farm was about to be hit by an even more alarming epidemic – epicureanism. Helen started the trend, throwing away her calorie-counter and serving up Beef Wellington for dad Tony's birthday. The fact that he had a heart attack a week or so later is surely unconnected, but, diagnosed with high cholesterol, Tony then became a guinea-pig for all sorts of experimental low-fat cookery.

He'd subsisted for years on soup (even, sometimes, shock, horror, tinned) and bread and cheese but now Pat swung into action with a skimmed-milk rice pudding while Jennifer wore a path from Home Farm with cholesterol-busting cakes and casseroles. Even Lilian, not known for her culinary skills, came good by popping to Underwoods Food hall to pick up some bags of nutritious seeds which she thought might be beneficial. Tony got his own back, though. Left to make the family's lunch while he was still unfit for farm work, he came up with a couple of truly adventurous sandwich fillings: Brie and mushroom or beef and avocado. *Bon appétit!*

AMBRIDGE VILLAGE SHOP – THEN AND NOW

Then		Now
Owned by Jack Woolley	→	Community shop
Counter service	→	Self-service
Grocery book	→	Shopping list on mobile phone
Same-day delivery service	→	DVDs
Mental arithmetic	→	EPOS scanner and till
Paid manager/ postmistress	→	Paid p/t manager/ postmistress and volunteer assistants
Tinned macaroni pudding	→	Fresh pasta
Blancmange	→	Pat Archer's yoghurt and ice cream

Bacon slicer	→	Credit card reader
Telephone box outside	→	Mobile phone top-ups
Pork scratchings	→	Pot Noodles
First-floor storeroom	→	Flat above the shop (current tenants: Rhys Williams and Fallon Rogers)
Bead curtain to stockroom	→	Door to stockroom
Neon sign (didn't last long)	→	Hand-painted sign

Still there: shop door with distinctive bell, separate post office with glass screen, American Tan tights (and possibly even popsox).

TEA POTTY

Stopping for TEA in Ambridge didn't necessarily mean a brew. As villagers sought to pioneer a new economy in 2008 that would enable the exchange of skills and produce, a new denomination of dosh was created, known as a TEA or Transition Equivalent in Ambridge. Each had a nominal value of 50 pence.

The theory sounded splendid. In practice there was chaos. The first sign of what lay ahead was a row between Lynda and Joe about how many TEAs each charged for lifts, with Lynda using her car and Joe a cart led by Bartleby. Then there were a series of IOUs, followed by a strong suspicion of forgery resulting in hyperinflation that rendered TEAs virtually valueless.

Eventually TEAs were phased out, although a simpler exchange scheme remained in the form of the Tea Cosy: a swap table in the shop after it became community-run in 2010.

EAT LOCAL

In 2009 Pip decided to eat only food grown within a five-mile radius of Brookfield during Lent. Although mother Ruth had grave doubts, Pip was ideally placed to create a tempting and varied menu.

Starters

Devilled eggs
(from Willow Farm)

Vegetable soup
(from assorted items in Bridge Farm vegetable boxes)

Main Courses

Venison casserole
(from Home Farm)

Pork en croute
(from Bridge Farm)

Roast lamb
(Hassett Hills lamb from Brookfield Farm)
(If she did the same today she could add pork meat balls with red pepper sauce – a ready meal from Tom Archer's range.)

Sweets

Ice cream
(from Bridge Farm)

Yoghurt
(from Bridge Farm)

Strawberries with cream
(from Home Farm) (from Bridge Farm)

Cheeseboard with Borsetshire Blue and Sterling Gold
(both handmade by Helen at Bridge Farm)

As the idea gained currency in Ambridge, adults observing this creative Lent discipline must have breathed a sigh of relief when they realised they weren't restricted to milk with their meals. There's cider produced by the Grundys and, pushing boundaries a bit, wine from Lower Loxley to accompany the all-local menu.

ST STEPHEN'S CHURCH – THEN AND NOW

Then		Now
Carved Bishop's chair	⟶	Modern equivalent – replaced after theft in 1996
Lectern	⟶	Ditto – in American white oak/beech
Brassware	⟶	Bars on the vestry window
King James Bible	⟶	Series Three Communion
Series Three Communion	⟶	New liturgy

Full set of pews	→	Some pews at back of church removed
Step up to church	→	Ramp for disabled access
Self-restraint	→	Church loo
Churchyard mown	→	Churchyard left wild as 'God's Acre'
Church choir led by Peter Marshal	→	Summer-resident peregrine falcons
Bishop Cyril	→	Archdeacon Rachel
Church postcards	→	Fair Trade goods

Still there: Flower Rota, bats, stained-glass window in memory of Phil Archer's first wife, Grace, font with carved heads of Edward I and Queen Eleanor of Castile, the Woolhay memorial.

A BLUE HILL REMEMBERED

Ambridge's landscape includes Lakey Hill, backdrop to events that embrace the momentous and the mundane.

- It's here that Dan Archer wooed his bride-to-be, the curiously named Doris Forrest, at the midsummer bonfire way back when.

- The tradition of building celebration bonfires there continued at regular intervals from that distant day until now, like the 2012 Jubilee beacon, an event that was four months in the planning. And every Easter a dawn service is held there.

- There are few of the village residents who haven't climbed the hill's grassy banks at one time or another, with a WI cake in their hand, a smile on their face and perhaps some home-brewed cider warming their insides.

- However, it's not solely a place for festivities. Shula and Mark – who called it 'the top of the world' – went there after they lost their first baby and yelled into the wind in fury and frustration. Shula frequently went there after Mark's death, to mourn and to bellow once more, this time about the injustice of his premature demise.

- In 1995, it took on darker hues still as the body of George Barford was found there by David and Phil. The retired gamekeeper keeled over after suffering a heart attack and his faithful dog Walt had stayed by the body. As Lakey Hill falls in the boundaries of Brookfield, David and Phil were checking hedges when they spotted the loyal dog.

Indeed, it's the acknowledged sanctuary that all the Archers retreat to when they have something on their minds. Phil and Elizabeth bumped into each other there in 1986, he to ponder the recent death of his father, she to dwell on the unfairness of life in general.

PHIL	You don't have exclusive rights on being fed up, you know.
ELIZABETH	At the moment it feels like it.
PHIL	I've been coming up here for almost fifty years. I'm surprised I haven't worn a path.
ELIZABETH	I hope I don't end up saying that at your age.
PHIL	Why, what's wrong with it?
ELIZABETH	I don't want to be the umpteenth generation of Archers fed up on Lakey Hill, that's why.
PHIL	I don't know. I find it quite a comforting thought.

ELIZABETH I'm 19 on Monday – and what have I got to look forward to? Two of us, both getting older, both having boring old family tea parties. I might as well be your age, mightn't I?

BORSETSHIRE BACKWATER

Glen Whitehouse, the Editor of *Borsetshire Life*, must by now have kissed goodbye to any ambitions he might have had to edit a more prestigious publication. Maybe it was Lynda Snell's letter to the Press Complaints Commission back in 2005 which stalled his career: Glen had not, she felt, given her renovated kitchen enough prominence in an article on home makeovers. She later became an occasional correspondent for the glossy, although, after getting off on the wrong foot, she at first had to hide behind the anagrammatical alias of 'Dylan Nells' to get a foot in the door.

Glen is known to despair of the 'tradition, tradition, tradition' ethos of the magazine's owners and fulminates about the so-called 'Sales and Development' department. His desired 'step-changes, brand-wise' such as wanting to retitle the magazine '*BLife*' have been dismissed out of hand, despite 'ad rev' soaring almost two per cent 'off the back of' his new features: 'Insider', 'Hot Goss' and the rest.

Despite – and because of – his concerns about *Borsetshire Life*'s trivial content, Jim Lloyd embarked on a career as a contributor and was commissioned for six articles on Borsetshire locals. Inevitably, he was outraged by the liberties taken with his carefully honed prose, not to mention Glen's ignorance of the proper use of the semi-colon. But what did Jim expect from a paper whose social pages are shamelessly entitled 'Borsetshire Bashes'?

SECRETS OF THE SHOW

Dan was an expert in growing carrots for the Flower and Produce Show. The secret was to plant them in a pot of sand. The results were magnificent and perfect for showing, though as Walter Gabriel pointed out (and Dan had to agree) they tasted horrible – 'like sunburnt chipboard'.

Pru Forrest frequently swept the board at the F and P Show. Her marrow rum was one such triumph. The recipe for this horticultural hooch:

> Halve a vegetable marrow, scoop seeds out of each half. Fill the hole with sugar, nick a small hole in the end and suspend halves over a jar. Fermentation takes places as the sugar filters through.

But beware; as husband Tom testified: 'Beautiful, it was, as long as you weren't planning on doing anything afterwards!'

Had it been entered for the Vegetable Olympics and not merely the annual Flower and Produce Show, Walter Gabriel's vegetable marrow would surely have tested positive for a banned substance. Dan Archer certainly had his suspicions when he came to view the monster specimen in August 1982:

WALTER	It's over here.
DAN	You've not cut it already?
WALTER	Twisted, Dan, not cut. You should always twist 'em off the vine. I got it under glass. Ripening... There! Feast your eyes on that!
DAN	I'll have to hand it to you, Walter. I reckon that's the biggest marrow I've ever seen... You've been feeding it, haven't you?
WALTER	(SLIGHT PAUSE) How do you know?
DAN	I can still see the needle mark in the stem. You've twisted it off on the wrong side.
WALTER	Doh! I'll have to cut that. Good, though, isn't it?
DAN	It is. What did you use? Glucose?

WALTER	(WITH HIS TRADEMARK CHUCKLE) Ordinary sugar and water. One end of a bit of wool in the jar, the other threaded through the stem, and Bob's your uncle. Keep it under glass to give it a good colour and come the show, you won't hear the wind for the gasps of astonishment echoing round Ambridge!

But it was not to be. Truly, crime does not pay, and when Tom Forrest also came on a tour of inspection…

TOM	Let's have a look.
WALTER	(QUICK) I'll do it, I'll do it! You've got to treat 'em with respect! (STRAINS UNDER CONSIDERABLE WEIGHT) There!
TOM	How much does it weigh? Give it here!
WALTER	Gently, gently! Hold your arms out! (SOFT EXPLOSION, AS OF SOMEONE THROWING UP INTO A BOWL OF RICE KRISPIES)
TOM	Eughk! Walter!
WALTER	What have you done? Me marrow!
TOM	I didn't do anything! It just burst! Look at me!

For anyone thinking of emulating Walter, the danger is this: the sugar had fermented inside the marrow once off the plant. The skin became brittle, the flesh rotted and gas built up inside – with inevitable consequences.

As the village clucked over Walter's underhand tactics, the last word was left to Walter's friend and frequent nemesis, Mrs P:

MRS P	At least all us honest folks'll be in with a chance.
WALTER	You didn't tell me you was growing vegetable marrows for the show!
MRS P	I wouldn't go telling you everything, Mr Gabriel, now would I?

In 1984 Pat was 'highly commended' for her informal table decoration while Jennifer seethed as an 'also ran'. Her mistake was leaving sections of the green oasis, used to hold the flowers in place, visible.

Winners of the memorial cup for the 'gentleman's buttonhole' category, sponsored from 2001 by Julia Pargetter in memory of Nelson Gabriel, include inaugural winner Peggy Woolley (who also won again in 2008), Freda Fry two years later and Jennifer Aldridge in 2004.

If Phil could depend on one crop to show each year then it was runner beans. For him it was not a case of attaching weights to the beans to make them grow longer and straighter – a technique used by both Bert Fry and Lynda Snell. No, he once confided to rival Bert, it was liberal amounts of Brookfield dung in the bean trench when the seedlings were planted out that made the difference.

In 2001, Bert and Joe were both determined to claim top spot in the 'men only' Victoria sponge section. Confronted by the basin and basic ingredients they floundered – and both turned to neighbour Kathy for advice. She was sworn to secrecy by each of them and she struggled to keep a straight face when they both turned up at the same time to receive cake-making tips. However, dark horse Christopher Carter had the lighter touch and won the first prize.

Two years later, Alistair was goaded into entering a cookery class by David, and discovered there was more to baking cakes than he at first thought. He discussed his culinary catastrophe with show veteran Bert:

ALISTAIR	I can't understand it. I followed the recipe to the letter.
BERT	Well you've used all the right ingredients. Although how you managed to get flour on that light fitting's anybody's guess.
ALISTAIR	I'll tidy up before Shula gets back.
BERT	Did you leave it in long enough?
ALISTAIR	You heard the timer beep.
BERT	Mmm. What about the temperature?
ALISTAIR	180 degrees. I put the cake in, set the dial –
BERT	Ooops, there's your mistake.
ALISTAIR	What?
BERT	You mean you didn't warm the oven up before you put it in?
ALISTAIR	Ah, didn't think it would make much difference.
BERT	It ent as easy as you thought, is it?

THE AMBRIDGE STING

Life in a village might become routine, but fortunately the residents of Ambridge have notched up numerous ways of putting some zing back into their daily lives. Take the 2003 nettle-eating contest as an example.

The frisson of excitement for the competition at The Bull was palpable, with Mike Tucker the acknowledged favourite thanks to his famously leathery hands. Eddie Grundy whipped up more fervour with an illicit betting scam, but that did nothing to detract from the event.

In the kitchen, Freda Fry played her part by dishing up nettle stew – although she had noticeably few takers.

Kirsty was the sole female entrant, but her efforts were thwarted when Eccles the peacock stole her nettles.

One contestant was disqualified for having ice cubes in his pocket, on hand to soothe his throbbing mouth.

When David Archer threw in the towel after three 2-foot lengths of nettle proved his limit, it seemed Mike had indeed won the day. No one noticed Bert Fry munching slowly but surely in the corner. And he was the unexpected victor, with the most unexpected victory speech:

> According to Hippocrates, a mixture of nettles, pigeon dung and cumin is very good for encouraging hair growth.

There was at least some consolation for the losers, with everything still to play for in the wife-carrying contest scheduled for the forthcoming village fete.

Should you be considering a nettle-eating championship, here are some top tips for winners:

1. Take your stem of nettles.

2. Pull off a leaf at its base, where it joins the stem, and rip it from the stalk.

3. Roll it in the same direction as the hairs on the leaf are pointing. (According to the most successful candidates, that stops you being stung.)

4. If in pain, wash down without chewing.

THE BULL – THEN AND NOW

'Playbar' – a coffee and milk bar for 'the young folk'	→	'The Bull Upstairs'
Jimmy Grange's skiffle group	→	Music nights with local bands
Local 'Talent Night'	→	Comedian Tug Fowler

Steak bar	→	Pies at the bar
Civil War-themed restaurant	→	Family restaurant
Nouvelle cuisine	→	Family fare
Cocktail cherries	→	Cocktail shaker
Jukebox	→	Widescreen TV
Fruit machine	→	Computers
Pints of mild	→	Foreign lagers – from the bottle
Pickled eggs	→	Thai-chilli-flavour crisps
Viking trophy for darts	→	Coffee machine behind the bar

behind the bar

Jack and Peggy's dog Turpin	→	Resident peacock, Eccles

Still there: the Ploughman's bar; the garden; hanging baskets; cribbage, darts and dominoes; the ghost of the Little Drummer Boy.

GUILTY PLEASURES

For most of us, there are areas of life that are best kept veiled. In Ambridge it is no different, with quirks and comforts that largely stay under the radar.

In common with many farmers, Brian likes to keep his old clothes in his wardrobe, no matter what their condition, where they can be readily accessed on a daily basis. This came to light when Jennifer once proposed a clear-out.

BRIAN	I haven't got any old clothes.
JENNIFER	You've got cupboards full of old clothes.
BRIAN	Those are clothes I love and need.

When the going got tough, Phil used to slip away into the orchard for a civilised heart-to-heart with his favourite sow, Molly.

Kirsty is a bit of a twitcher in her spare time. She's seen the kingfisher that's eluded many Ambridge residents and heard a reed warbler while hanging out in the hide at Arkwright Lake.

Walter enjoyed a glass – or four – of his own home-made beer while Joe indulges in a pint or more of cider.

For Lilian, there are few days that pass without her indulging in a gin and tonic and ciggie. When she and Eddie were coerced into giving up drink for Lent they fell back on the naturally devious sides of their natures and went to great lengths to cheat throughout.

Shula loves chocolate so much that after giving it up for Lent in 2000, and being reduced to sniffing chocolate-scented candles, she declared to Jill she would never stop eating it again. Her sole comfort had been watching Alistair suffer by giving up alcohol at the same time.

… AND A CUDDLY TOY

Partners and friends come and go, but a stuffed toy remains a stout companion in good times and bad.

Fallon has a badger called Binky.

Keira loves a rabbit called Hopalong.

Emma still has an unnamed bear sent to her in hospital by Jolene after her car accident in 2001.

When she met Mike, Vicky proudly showed Mike her collection of thirty-three teddies. Her favourite is Mr Bubbles, and that became her pet name for him.

Elizabeth won't part with a teddy bear called Frosty, named after the song 'Frosty the Snowman', given to her by Shula for her sixth birthday.

Nigel remained fond of a teddy bear called Tiddles throughout his life, even though it had replacement eyes. And he had many bears to choose from, as the mini-museum of toys kept in a room at Lower Loxley testifies. In it there are two other bears – Monty and Growler, who dates from 1910 – Mickey the Monkey, a full-size rocking horse called Dobbin, his sister Camilla's dolls, Punch and Judy show puppets and an array of toy soldiers.

HOMESPUN HOMILIES FROM THE HEART AND HEARTH

'This and better might, but this and worse will never.'

Walter, quoting his old Granny, to Doris Archer. Luckily Dan was on hand to translate. He explained it was the equivalent of 'This won't buy me a new hat/get the baby bathed' and other old-time favourites. In modern parlance, Just Do It!

'If it doesn't hurt a little when you lose
there's no point in playing.'
Alistair, about gambling

'A true Pargetter never does things by halves.'
Nigel, about losing at gambling

'You can always lose what you've got trying to get more, and end up with nothing.'
Norah McAuley's take on life more usually expressed with the proverb 'a bird in the hand…'

'Never give your number to a girl you are not interested in.'
Jealous Jazzer revealed his key to success with women after Harry was plagued by calls

'Bigger isn't necessarily better.'
Ralph Bellamy, in this case, about farming

'I've always made my own bed. I just wish it wasn't so lumpy.'
Mo Travis, trying to lure Neil Carter into her clutches

'You can't fight your genes.'
Lillian to Peggy after keep-fit Sid's demise

'I've got hidden shallows, me.'
Jazzer, reassuringly, to Ed

'Easy to get nothing wrong if you never do nothing in the first place.'
Jolene's wise words to have-a-go Kenton

'Central heating has a great bearing on a marriage.'
Dan Archer

'Everything tastes better when it's been made with love.'
Doris Archer

'Sighing is the ancient art of spreading sadness
all around.'
Brian to a heavy-hearted Jenny,
following Polly Perks's sudden death

'Eddie Grundy! What have you done this time?'
Clarrie, often

STAR QUALITY

A horde of celebrities have beaten a path to Ambridge over the years, often in connection with the village fete.

Humphrey Lyttleton	Band leader, opened the village fete in 1957, momentous for being the afternoon that Phil fell for Jill.
Richard Todd	Well-known film star of the era, opened Ambridge fete in 1962, having been filming nearby.
Gilbert Harding	An irascible celebrity who appeared regularly on *What's My Line* before his death in 1960, bought a lavender bag from the adoring Mrs P when he visited Ambridge.
Antony Gormley	Turned up to the fete in 2009 after Ambridge residents failed to win a place on his Trafalgar Square plinth One & Other. As a response, Lynda instituted a village plinth at the fete and Molly Button dressed as a mushroom was the plinth winner, fighting off stiff competition. The artist wasn't the judge on this occasion but marked his day by winning a hand-knitted bobble hat at one of the stalls.

Colin Dexter	The crime writer who created Inspector Morse opened the fete in 2010.
Anneka Rice	Organised the painting and redecoration of the village hall over three days in 1993, mirroring the popular TV programme of the era called *Challenge Anneka.*
Alan Titchmarsh	Judged the Ambridge entrants in the National Gardens Scheme contest held in 2003.
Terry Wogan	Was at the Grey Gables golf course for a celebrity match in 1989. Pru Forrest gave him a welcoming pot of damson jam.
John Peel	Came to Ambridge in 1991 when BBC Radio One organised its disc jockeys' lunch at Grey Gables.
Griff Rhys Jones	The comedian and writer was drawn into Lynda Snell's campaign to re-instate the Cat and Fiddle, Ambridge's second and now defunct pub, in July 2004. Thank goodness the campaign failed. With a lunchtime menu featuring black pudding sandwiches and a reputation for spreading 'Cat and Fiddle tummy', it was more hazard than hostelry.

Village visitors have even included royalty, with Princess Margaret dropping by in 1984, and the Duke of Westminster and the Duchess of Cornwall arriving in 2011.

And out of the village…

Dame Edna Everage	Was at a local theatre in 1988 and Lynda and Robert got tickets. Inevitably, Lynda was summoned to the stage, to be ritually insulted by the star. However, she saw it differently, believing: 'I've just upstaged a mega-star. And it was more than a mere victory, it was a complete humiliation.'
Zandra Rhodes	The cricketer, settled a dispute between Sid and Jolene Perks as they were watching the cup final of a village cricket competition held at Lords in September 2007.
Mike Gatting	The cricketer settled a dispute between Sid and Jolene Perks as they were watching the cup final of a village cricket competition held at Lords in September 2007.
Lord Lichfield	Took the photos at Shula and Mark's wedding on 21 September 1985 at Netherbourne Hall. (Lichfield was 'a friend' of Lord Netherbourne.)

FAMILY LIFE

AT THE HEART OF Ambridge life there is the extended Archer family, bigger than it has ever been and with a more perplexing dynamic. Sometimes it's perceptible that family members young and old mirror DNA, a powerful glue that ensures there is always substance over style. At other highly charged moments when relationships break down, they appear like hostile strangers to one another. But it takes more than one family to make a village, and Ambridge is marked by the progress of other families, too, including the Grundys, the Tuckers and, whisper it softly, the Horrobins.

Between them all, there are more politics than Parliament. There's sibling rivalry gone large between the Grundys that frequently threatens to pull the family to pieces, despite Clarrie's best efforts to keep them unified. Susan Carter is the 'black sheep' of the Horrobin family, with her largely sensible and law-abiding ways. Meanwhile, Jennifer, who risked casting herself out of the family circle by becoming an unmarried mother, proved there is always the glowing hope of redemption.

The problems of parenting have stayed the same down the years. As a young man, Phil told father Dan he didn't want to be tied to the farm for the rest of his life. Years later David spoke on similar lines to a frustrated Phil. Both were confronted by daughters whose attitudes and ambitions varied considerably from their own.

In a village like Ambridge there's a strong chance young and wilful residents will alight on rôle models outside the immediate family. It's a formula that's worked well, as those Grundy boys would testify.

YOU CAN CHOOSE YOUR FRIENDS...

But there's a skeleton in every family's closet.

Joe Grundy's elder son, Alf, is a black sheep, with his past spells in prison for handling stolen copper wire. Latterly it seems the only thing he can be accused of is general misanthropy and strange food fads, though an aversion to pastry is a pretty serious offence in Ambridge, where most festivities have a heavy dependence on sausage rolls.

Vicky has had trouble in the past with her embarrassing stepdad, Eric, who has an annoying beard, favours shorts and is happiest when he's talking about caravanning. The fact that he made a friend of the generally disliked Neville Booth when attending Vicky's wedding to Mike Tucker says it all.

When Elizabeth Cartwright visited in 1977, Jennifer felt put down by Brian's sister's superior knowledge and freely voiced opinions on the running of the farm – although this didn't stop Liz being made one of Kate's godparents later the same year. Perhaps, though, she proved to be the Bad Fairy at the christening, because she's never been heard of, or from, again.

Shula doesn't have much luck with her in-laws. She was dreading the appearance of Mark Hebden's sister, Joanna, a dumpy redhead, as bridesmaid in her wedding photos, though to say this influenced Shula's decision to call off the wedding first time round is probably going too far. Her second husband Alistair's sister Fiona poses a different sort of problem.

Briskly washing her hands of their father Jim, Shula dispatched him to The Stables to recover from a broken leg, a stay he thoroughly enjoyed – which was more than could be said for Shula. Jim moved to the village for good in 2009, and seemed bent on a campaign of mischievously tormenting her, though their relationship has softened of late.

Meanwhile, Shula's first set of in-laws, Reg and Bunty Hebden, tottered on precariously into their 90s and, as their daughter Joanna lives some distance away, Shula nobly took on some of the burden of care for them. Her relations with Bunty had mellowed (she described Bunty's wedding outfit as coming 'from Rent-A-Tent') and though she finds former solicitor Reg dull, he somehow inspired an interest in the law in grandson Daniel. Following Bunty's death in February 2013, Reg has now moved up north to be closer to Joanna, to Shula's undoubted relief.

THERE'S LOTS IN A NAME

PHIL — If it was a boy, for example, we could call him George Daniel... or Daniel George... then both grandpas would be pleased.

GRACE — (SMILE) Looking ahead a bit, aren't we?

PHIL	On second thoughts I'm not much for either of those names, are you?
GRACE	No. Definitely not. Something like Antony or Jeremy.
PHIL	Jeremy I like...
GRACE	Well, George and Daniel are right out. If we had a girl I wouldn't dream of calling her Doris or Helen... we don't have to consider the grandparents to that extent, do we surely?

Poignantly, this was the conversation between Phil and Grace Archer the night before her tragic death in September 1955. After looking after a friend's baby, Grace had finally melted and agreed that she and Phil should start trying for a baby sooner rather than later. It wasn't to be, of course, though Phil later went on to have four children with Jill.

Not that naming those children came easily either. Having stunned the family with their radical choices of Shula and Kenton for the twins, the choice of David for Phil and Jill's second son might have seemed a return to convention, but for the fact that Jill considered the name Blane till someone told her it meant 'pimple'. (In fact it's derived from the Gaelic *Blain* and means 'yellow'.) David managed to hold his own with his more unusually named siblings however, being nicknamed 'Snowball' for most of his childhood owing to his very blond hair.

Other name-debates have included...

George Edward Grundy	Will got his way on the first name, calling his son after his mentor, George Barford, but Emma cunningly suggested Edward as a middle name. Thought to be a nod to grandfather Eddie, in fact it was more a signal to Will's brother Ed, whom she fervently believed was the baby's father.
Keira Susan Grundy	Though exotic enough for Ambridge, little Keira could have had an even more unusual name. During pregnancy, Emma toyed with Skye or Summer – even though, as Clarrie pointed out prosaically, the baby would be born in the spring. Though Emma had favoured so many names beginning with 'S', Susan wasn't among them, so grandma Susan Carter was delighted and surprised to be told the baby would take her name too – as a middle name.
Bethany Claire Tucker	When first pregnant, Vicky wondered about Dorothy, her grandmother's name, if the baby was a girl. As debates intensified and the baby's sex was confirmed, there was one thing both she and Mike could agree on. 'Daisy' made them think of his cows – so that was off the list. Finally they chose the names they kept coming back to – they also both like the diminutive, Beth.
Philippa Rose Archer	Pip was named after a grandparent, her grandfather, Phil – though he was slow to get the connection when first introduced to the baby in the maternity ward. Pip's middle name, Rose, is after Ruth's favourite aunt.

Joshua Matthew Archer	Unable to mine the family tree any further – Shula had grabbed the name Daniel, and John (another Archer name) had been used by Pat and Tony for their firstborn – Ruth and David decided to go out on a limb in naming their first son. They returned to the fold with their next child, though.
Benjamin David Archer	When miracle baby Ben (born after Ruth's cancer) arrived in 2002, David had a wobble when, having settled on the first name, Ruth suggested a family name for a second. Thinking she was going to land their son with the name Solomon, after her father, he was relieved and pleased when it turned out it was his name that was to be perpetuated.
Phoebe Tucker	After her birth in a tepee at Glastonbury and with the prospect of a naming ceremony on Lakey Hill rather than a christening, expectations were not high for Kate's baby's name. Rainbow appeared to be favourite, and there was much relief – not least for Phoebe's dad, Roy – when Kate revealed a more traditional streak, naming her daughter after her own great-great-grandmother.
Noluthando Grace and Sipho Madikane	Nolly's name means 'love' and Sipho's 'gift' in Xhosa.

Emma and Christopher Carter	Susan might be seen as giving her children aspirational names – Emma was named after the Jane Austen novel she'd read at school and she was firm about never shortening Christopher's name. It's only Alice who's contracted it to 'Chris'.
William George Grundy	On the day that Prince Charles and Lady Diana Spencer announced their engagement, Clarrie mournfully sashayed round the family living room to the strains of 'Someday My Prince Will Come'. Would Eddie ever get round to proposing? But by the end of the year, they were married, and when their son was born in February 1983, there was never any doubt that, with her eye still firmly on the Royal couple, the Grundy son and heir would be named after the second in line to a rather bigger throne.

GEORGE'S NINE LIVES

By the time George Grundy was eight, he had already clocked up some significant lucky escapes. As a toddler, a CD rack fell on him, landing him in Accident and Emergency, and during the intimidation of the Brookfield Archers he was first nearly crushed against a gate by a herd of stampeding bullocks. Then, a month later, he went missing at the time of the barn blaze – only to be found safely occupied with Josh and a calving cow. Who knows what will befall him now he's doing karate…

HORSEPOWER

In breaking his collarbone in a fall from his father's horse, Topper, in 2012, Freddie Pargetter was keeping up a fine family tradition. His late father Nigel broke his collarbone in 2002 in an ill-advised quad bike race with Kenton, while in a nasty fall at a horse show in East Anglia forty years earlier, Freddie's great-aunt Christine broke her collarbone and two ribs and badly wrenched her knee.

In the wider village, collarbones have regularly cracked. Clive Lawson-Hope found himself concussed and with a broken collarbone after a fall at the Hollerton Point-to-Point in 1952, while more recently Caroline Sterling's fall at the Lower Loxley Team Chase landed her in Accident and Emergency with a suspected broken collarbone – though it turned out to be her arm which was broken. And at Home Farm Brian had to scramble around to find replacement cover one summer when one of the proposed student helpers broke his collarbone when he came off a mountain bike.

'GRUNDY ENTERPRISES... HOW CAN I HELP YOU?'

The fortunes of the Grundy family have ebbed rather than flowed over the years. Their family exploits to finance an extra pint or two have raised as many smiles as scowls. When they confounded efforts to oust them from Grange Farm in the 1990s, there was implied triumph around their activities, sometimes conducted at the margins of legitimacy. But when their feverish efforts were to fend off bankruptcy in the millennium there was a sense of doomed desperation about their multi-tasking.

Joe was a farmer until he was evicted from Grange Farm in 2000, with a side line in field rental for car boot sales, pop festivals and caravan sites. Since then he has kept pigs, sold wood to raise extra cash and undertaken various odd jobs despite his advancing years. With his trusty pony Bartleby, he has latched on to providing carbon-free transport to the ecologically wary as a way of supplementing his pension.

More recently still, Joe has developed his mystic side, blessing what he termed 'sacred oaks' before impregnating them with mistletoe berries. Most potential customers were deterred by the fact his Druid's garb was very evidently one of Clarrie's bed sheets and that his self-confessed inspiration was Harry Potter. With son Eddie, he has provided numerous turkeys for Ambridge households at Christmas.

It is Eddie who has taken diversification to new levels, inspired to take on all manner of projects in pursuit of a quick buck. Somehow, though, he always ends up working long and hard for uncertain reward.

He began working life with some degree of normality. Eddie was working for Hollerton Plant Hire in 1979, without distinguishing himself on the ditch-clearing operations. It helped to bridge the financial gap he suffered because Joe refused to hand over cash for the work he did on the farm. His career there came to an abrupt end when the manager found out Eddie was making liberal use of the equipment during evenings and weekends to further his own private interests.

In his twenties, Eddie rolled up his sleeves when he realised he could not live on the £10.50 a week in supplementary benefits he was entitled to after being sacked, together with the miserly amount given to him by his father. He became a lorry driver for a short spell until Joe realised he couldn't manage without him and finally promised to pay him a living wage.

Attempts to make fast cash selling shampoo made from soap provided by Nelson Gabriel in 1980 were, predictably, doomed to failure. It was the same story when it came to his career as a Country and Western star, partnering Jolene and her then husband Wayne Tucson. No amount of rhinestone could add glitter to that career choice, as it turned out. Disillusioned and flat broke, Eddie had to turn back to what he knew best.

As the rural economy continued to freefall, Eddie began selling chipped hedge trimmings at £3 a bag – and it soon became clear that where there's mulch there's brass. By 2000, he was selling manure at 70 pence a bag or £25 a load and was the superintendent of compost piles dotted across Willow Farm, much to Neil's consternation.

With Lynda's help, he created leaflets advertising 'Eddie's Vintage – the fertility power pack for your prizewinning blooms', and it was soon in demand at car boot sales across the area. He further supplemented his income by making garden ornaments, water features and laying patios. Indeed, his ornaments, ranging from mooning gnomes to the Beast of Ambridge, have been a surprisingly profitable side line down the decades.

Before the modern era, when foreign students were brought in, he helped with potato picking and fruit harvests. There has always been seasonal work for Eddie at Christmas, too, with the provision of holly, mistletoe and trees. He has retained the cutting rights at Grange Farm, although when pressed he will only admit that the festive greenery comes from 'round and about'.

He has provided rabbits for those with a taste for pie as well as the odd illicitly killed pheasant. Then there's Grundy cider, infamous rather than renowned, and home-brewed apple brandy. He once even undertook a short but lucrative spell as a burger flipper, working from a van on the Borchester bypass.

By 2002, Eddie was on the lookout for landscaping jobs undertaken from behind the wheel of a new JCB, ostensibly bought for Ed but mostly used by an excitable Eddie. In fact, he was much more interested in practising his 'disco diggers' routine with mate Fat Paul for the village fete than using it for work. Cornering and braking took its toll on Lynda Snell's paddock, which was his rehearsal ground of choice.

Selling condemned meat in 2004 wasn't his finest hour. He worked long and hard on the vine wires at Lower Loxley in an attempt to recoup some of his losses after that caper.

Despite all this feverish activity, money still had a habit of drying up in the Grundy household. When things were tight in 2009 Eddie asked the vicar to mention in his sermon the 'odd job' services available at Keeper's Cottage. After all, he reasoned, it would save on the costs of advertising in the parish magazine.

Throughout he has always been on hand to help other farmers with milking or lambing. In 2011, he worked three nights a week in the lambing sheds during a busy spring at Brookfield. Then there's fencing and logging, two other staples for under-employed agricultural hands like himself. Latterly he has found work at Borchester market as a livestock handler, and does regular milking work at Brookfield.

Clarrie is also versatile as she struggles to keep the family finances in the black. She's been successful as a barmaid, milkmaid and ice-cream maker but her attempts as a stay-at-home mum to make money as an envelope stuffer came to grief when a young William sold the titillating underwear catalogues that she was meant to be dispatching to his mates. In any event, the payment cheque from the lingerie company subsequently bounced. Things went from bad to worse when the company representative turned up to collect his glossy leaflets, to find that Joe had shredded them for pig bedding.

It hasn't been entirely the same story for Eddie and Clarrie's sons, however. Ed's roguish ways culminated in a scheme to grow cannabis with Jazzer. On the pretext of fixing up an old Ford Escort that he bought for £300, Ed purloined garage space at Bridge Farm, much against Tony's better judgement. When Tony discovered alien tools in the barn that appeared for all the world to be stolen goods, he was convinced Ed and Jazzer were up to no good. Ed innocently explained he and Jazzer were fixing tools for people and had even fixed some of Tony's. What with their innocent explanations and Pat's subsequent admonishment, Tony was duly chastened. It was six weeks later that he discovered a stash of some 200 marijuana plants being nurtured in the barn loft for sale and consumption by the pair. With some satisfaction, he watched them destroy the plants by putting them through the very shredder Ed had mended to get on Tony's good side.

These days it is much more a case of 'rock steady Ed', with him mindful of his responsibilities as a family man. Struggling as a tenant farmer, he has learned how to vaccinate badgers against TB on a course run by the Department of Environment, Food and Rural Affairs, at a time when the government actively favoured badger culls. He's also set up a sheep-shearing business with his mate Jazzer.

Meanwhile, William is a gamekeeper on the estate and a fine shot.

If the brothers' working lives seem comparatively stable, the same can't be said of their love lives. The warring boys became two points of a love triangle with Emma – once married to William, now Ed's partner – at its apex, driving a long-standing wedge between them.

TEN THINGS I HATE ABOUT YOU

The extraordinary sight of Ed and Will Grundy shaking hands on the latter's 30th birthday in 2013 was sufficient to bring the village to a standstill. For a dozen years, the brothers have been the worst of enemies, much to mother Clarrie's consternation. The barely or rarely masked hostility has caused heartache for Joe too, who sees history repeating itself, with the boys' father Eddie and uncle Alf at loggerheads all their adult lives.

Most people had assumed Ed and Will's relationship was broken beyond repair. Well, the future is brighter now the lads have bowed to pressure from partners and parents to at least share the same air with each other on high days and holidays. However, nothing can erase the troubled history that's brought them to this, most of it with Emma at its heart. She conducted on-off affairs with them both, to devastating effect. She even married 'stuck in the mud' William and had his baby. But the lure of 'bad boy' Ed always proved too great. Accordingly, William hates Ed because:

1. Ed nearly killed Emma by driving too fast in 2001. It happened on a night William and Emma were on a date. Emma left William and joined Ed in his brother's 'borrowed' car because she wanted to go home early.

2. He slept with William's wife-to-be Emma on her hen night in 2004.

3. Ed gave Emma secret driving lessons the following year.

4. With a carefree approach to life, Ed has always been able to make Emma laugh.

5. Three times Ed has broken up Emma and William's relationship.

6. Ed has travelled around Europe while dependable William stayed put.

7. Everybody was worried when drug-addled Ed went missing for months, especially his mother Clarrie. Just another example of Ed drawing attention to himself, William believed.

8. Ed has landed up working back at Grange Farm, the loss of which devastated the family in 2000. It's something that's brought undue glory to Ed, William feels.

9. He suspects Ed has poached game from the estate.

10. William's son George loves Ed's cows.

Ed hates William because:

1. He feels William, the older of the pair, has always looked down on him.

2. A DNA test proved conclusively that William is George's real dad, although Emma had cause for doubt. Ed wishes it were him.

3. William shook him warmly by the throat, almost killing him, in 2008.

4. William always seems to be 'a golden boy', receiving a bumper insurance pay out after Ed crashed William's car and inheriting money too.

5. He's boring.

6. A phone call from William to prospective employers ended Ed and Emma's dream of a new life in France.

7. Whenever there's a problem between them, William threatens to get the police or a solicitor to sort it out, making out he has the law on his side all the time.

8. Ed feels Eddie continually takes William's side.

9. Ed and Emma must take William's maintenance money for George each week, a matter of deep humiliation for proud but cash-strapped Ed.

10. Even though he is now married to Nic and they are starting a family together, Ed suspects William still holds a flickering candle for Emma.

THE SUBLIME TO THE RIDICULOUS

Perhaps the kindest way to describe the Horrobin family is rainbow colourful. There's Kylie, who is warm, bright and loved by everyone who knows her. That she is the daughter of the errant Clive is a genealogical mystery that's not lost on granddad Bert.

BERT	I'm not one for books, neither was your nana Ivy.
KYLIE	I shouldn't think she had time, with six kids.
BERT	She was so proud of you, Kylie, the first one in the family to go to a university.
KYLIE	Loads of people go these days.
BERT	You're going to make something of your life...

KYLIE	Only if I get a job.
BERT	... whilst your father, who was the apple of your nana's eye, he has led a life of ruin...

Clive's sister Susan is hardworking, his brother Keith has a tendency towards law breaking while Gary is something of a layabout.

Then there's his second sister, Tracy, fuelled by high drama. When she left partner Den she moved in with Susan and Neil with her children Chelsea and Brad. After she finally agreed to share a home with dad Bert, Neil was only too pleased to help shift her stuff from Den's flat.

However, her sense of theatre had them hiding in his van among six large helium balloons muffling dire warnings that Den would rearrange Neil's face if they were caught. With her nerves in tatters, Tracy lit up a cigarette shortly before a loud bang shattered the silence.

NEIL	Was that a shotgun?
TRACY	No, my ciggie's burst a balloon. Oh, Chelsea will go mad.
NEIL	Never mind Chelsea, you nearly gave me a heart attack.

Slowly Den approached the van after the rumpus, compelling a terrified Neil to open the window. He wasn't about to batter Neil or threaten Tracy, though. He simply wanted to offer some money to the children.

WISE WORDS

When journalist Jennifer was living as a single mum in Bristol after having Adam in 1967, she met her father Jack for a heart-to-heart.

No, she was not the victim of sly remarks. 'One or two raised eyebrows to begin with, I've had far less comment than if I'd stayed on here in Ambridge.'

No, she didn't have a relationship on the horizon, nor was there likely to be one for the time being. 'Can't say I've improved my chances of getting married.'

No, she wasn't depriving baby Adam of a father and a name. 'Don't worry, he will have both, all in due course.'

But yes, she did want to know about family matters and was anxious to hear about how Doris Archer was faring after breaking her wrist when an attacker struck at Brookfield. (Later Doris won £250 from the Criminal Injuries Compensation Board.)

'One thing about the Archer family, things never stop happening, do they?' remarked Jennifer presciently.

'No, never,' agreed Jack. 'Always summat up with summat.'

FOR AND AGAINST

When Jennifer became pregnant at a time when illegitimacy still held considerable stigma, her family and friends fell broadly into two categories: supporters and detractors.

Supporters

- Her mainstay was granddad Dan Archer, who reminded the rest of the fulminating family that she was 'a human being in trouble'. He feared recriminations from close family would drive Jennifer to having a termination – in the year the Abortion Act became law in Britain.

- Aunt Laura, the most worldly wise of the family, was the first family member to be told about the pregnancy by Jenny and quickly offered her a home.

- Jill, her aunt, who already had children of her own.

- Rev Matthew Wreford, who gently refused Jennifer's sweetly worded entreaties to intervene with her parents. 'I'm in a terrible mess. And yet it's my own fault and I'm going to face up to it, but sooner or later my parents have got to be told and that's just something I can't bring myself to do.

And I wonder, Mr Wreford, would you tell them?' Without moralising, he urged her to speak to Peggy and Jack herself.

- Peggy, eventually.
- Sister Lilian was also unshockable and supportive.

Detractors

- Doris Archer, who believed the baby's father – initially a secret but later proved to be absent cowman Paddy Redmond – should be made to marry Jennifer.
- Jack, her father, who instantly wanted to throw her out.
- Peggy's mother, Mrs P, who left The Bull, where she and Jenny both lived, because of the perceived shame of the pregnancy. Although Peggy implored her to change her mind, Mrs P insisted: 'If I says a thing, I means it'. Only months later, after Adam was born, did she come around to the idea, arriving in Ambridge on the bus to bring him a handmade romper suit.
- Tony, her younger brother, was noticeably reticent.

'FUNNY CREATURES WOMEN, AREN'T THEY?'

George Fairbrother gave some curious 'fatherly' advice to a young Phil after he came close to compromising his relationship with girlfriend Grace through inappropriate closeness with poultry keeper Jane Maxwell. Fairbrother, who was Grace's father, made his fortune in plastics. Perhaps that explains his smooth touch.

GEORGE	Ah well, funny creatures women, aren't they?
PHIL	Yes, life would be dreary without them though, I think.
GEORGE	I see what you mean. Ah, they are all right as long as you don't try to understand them. That's when you land yourself in trouble.
PHIL	I couldn't agree more.
GEORGE	Take Grace now, about the poultry. She's cooled off a bit on that job, hasn't she?
PHIL	Well, to be honest, Sir, she has cooled off quite a lot.
GEORGE	I'm not surprised. You should tell her off, you know.
PHIL	I already have in a nice way.

GEORGE Nice way be hanged. Tell her off in a nasty way. She'll take a lot more notice. In any case, she's not experienced enough for the job, is she? Always talking about wanting a job then when she's got one she neglects it.

PHIL Well, it isn't everybody's idea of fun, poultry keeping.

GEORGE She shouldn't have taken on the job. You want to talk to her like a Dutch uncle, my lad. She'll take more notice of you than she does of me.

PHIL Oh, I wouldn't say that.

GEORGE Well I would. I think you'd better ring up the Harper Adams College and see if they've got someone as good as Jane Maxwell.

PHIL Right.

GEORGE Ah, but Philip.

PHIL Yes, Sir.

GEORGE This time choose someone who is nice and plain and ordinary looking. Someone with the face like the back of a bus.

(PHIL LAUGHS)

GEORGE	I don't think it pays to mix glamour and poultry, if you see what I mean.
PHIL	I think I get what you're driving at, Sir.

DREAMY TEENS

Awkward teenagers are the bedrock on which the Archer family is built. But what a difference a generation makes. Shula was quirky in her teenage rebellion, while Pip is much more robust. It allowed Phil to show deft parenting while David floundered in a fury prompted mostly by his daughter being entirely immune to his influence.

Today's Shula would surely wince if she had sufficient total recall to bring up this moony exchange with father Phil in her bedroom, when she was approaching her 15th birthday and feeling under the weather:

PHIL	You worried about something, Shula?
SHULA	Worried? Yes... about the whole universe...
PHIL	Rather a lot to take on, isn't it?
SHULA	That's the trouble... I have the spirit. It's the flesh that's frail...
PHIL	You're as strong as a horse.

SHULA So you may think. They've said that about many a soul. And then, suddenly, pouf!

PHIL Pouf?

SHULA Like a snuffed candle flame... the fluttering heart... just... stopped.

PHIL Your heart isn't fluttering and it's not suddenly going to stop... pouf.

SHULA How can you know? How can you be sure? How can any of us know?

PHIL Because doctors are trained to know these things. Your medical reports have always been first class.

SHULA Poor, deluded Dad. I lie in bed and I hear my heart beating and I like to think – well, I know – it just can't go on like that day after day, year after year.

PHIL Don't see why not. Millions of hearts do.

SHULA Oh dear, I thought you'd understand.

PHIL Oh, I do, dear, I'm terribly sorry for you... in the circumstances.

SHULA Thank you, Dad... What circumstances?

PHIL Lilian's just rung up to see whether you'd be free to ride one of their new ponies this week. I said I'd ring her back. She will be as distressed to hear of your desperate condition as I am.

The temptation of riding a new pony facilitated a quick recovery.

In contrast, compare the blood-and-thunder exchange between David and Pip, aged 16. Having discovered from one of her friends that Pip's new boyfriend, Jude Simpson, was 29, David was bursting with self-righteous parental concern and began an argument that has echoed in a similar format through homes across the country over the years.

PIP You had no right to go interrogating my friends.

DAVID You lied to us, Pip, that's what really upsets me.

PIP Because I knew you would give me a hard time, that's why, which is exactly what you are doing, so well done, Dad, predictable as ever.

Afterwards they can't have a conversation that doesn't end in an argument.

PIP	You are such a hypocrite. You are loads older than Mum, and that's fine.
DAVID	That is totally different. We are eight years apart. And your mum was a lot older than 16 when we got together.
PIP	I'm nearly 17.
DAVID	He's not right for you, Pip.
PIP	How can you say that, you haven't even met him?
DAVID	I don't need to.
PIP	It doesn't matter how intelligent he is, it doesn't matter that we have the same sense of humour and that we like the same things.
DAVID	Pip, men of his age have a different outlook on life from someone your age.
PIP	This might come as surprise to you Dad, but he really likes me.
DAVID	I worry about you. We both do. We don't want you to get hurt.
PIP	No one is going to get hurt. And anyway it is up to me, so please stop trying to control my life.

David maintained his hostility to Jude, to the point where even Ruth called him Neanderthal. When Jude – nicknamed Grandpa

Simpson by Pip's younger brother Josh on account of his mature years – upturned a quad bike with Pip on the back her father seized the opportunity and banned him from the farm.

If only he had waited, time would have played its hand and ended the romance. Pip's plans to quit college and travel the world with Jude all came to naught when he went off to New York without her.

CAR-FULLY DOES IT

Since he's had a licence, Eddie has had an abiding interest in cars. Few have been run-of-the-mill motors that most people find on their drive. Here are three that bore the hallmark that's so distinctively Grundy.

In 1986, there was the powder blue Ford Capri he'd bought for £380. In a dozen years on the road it had clocked up just 30,000 miles. With a heady combination of leopard-skin seat covers and furry dice, Eddie wasn't fazed that the CB aerial on the top was defunct. After all, it had a modern cassette player inside. It was a prized possession for many years until he was forced to part with it when money got tight.

Following the loss of Grange Farm, he became a man with a van after setting up his own landscaping business. It wasn't the wording on the side that set the van apart: 'Eddie's Garden Products – Landscape Gardener, Garden Makeovers'. It was the picture on the back of two copulating pigs that brought a flush to Clarrie's cheeks.

The pair of partnering pigs was in the range of concrete garden ornaments produced and sold by Eddie. That didn't make it any less embarrassing for Clarrie when she was taken to the supermarket in the van to do the weekly shop. Her protestations came to nothing after Eddie insisted the depiction of the pigs brought in new business.

But in 2010 she was considerably firmer with him when he had her name painted on the front of his new van, above an allegedly abstract drawing. As they say in the films, any resemblance to people living or dead was purely accidental. As she approached the van she immediately liked the drawing of a ferret on its side, accompanying Eddie's slogan: Quick as a ferret. But when she saw the bonnet, with her name and the graphic beside it, she was furious and demanded it was repainted immediately.

CLARRIE	I don't care what you've got planned for this afternoon.
EDDIE	(APPEALS) Clarrie...
CLARRIE	As soon as you've dropped me off, you can go back and get that picture painted out.
EDDIE	How many more times, Clarrie. It is not meant to be you.
CLARRIE	Never mind what it's meant to be.
EDDIE	It's a smiley sun. That's why it's got a round face.
CLARRIE	A smiley sun that just happens to have my name over the top.
EDDIE	That doesn't make it a picture of you.

CLARRIE	Listen, Eddie. Your ketchup bottle says tomato on the label. And what's that red thing just below it? It's not a plum is it?
EDDIE	That's different.
CLARRIE	The front of this van says Clarrie. In great big letters.
EDDIE	Yeah. I thought you'd be pleased.
CLARRIE	Pleased?
EDDIE	I was calling the van after you.
CLARRIE	With a picture that makes me look fat and stupid.
EDDIE	Clarrie...
CLARRIE	And what about my hair? It looks awful.
EDDIE	It's not hair. It's the sun's rays.
CLARRIE	I'm not a fool, Eddie.
EDDIE	I know that, love.
CLARRIE	So stop treating me like one.
EDDIE	I'm not. I wouldn't do that to you.
CLARRIE	I mean it, Eddie. You get that picture painted out. And quick. Otherwise you and me are going to fall out big time.

LOVE HURTS

Creating a new family is a momentous step and when older father Mike and ageing new mum Vicky took the plunge there was laughter and tears.

Initially it seemed the prospect of a new baby was nothing more than an impossible dream. Feeling irritable and out-of-sorts, Vicky believed she was going through 'the change' and mourned the passing of her fertile years. Confidante Lynda was on hand to comfort her that, in Lynda's case, once 'all that' was behind her, life took on a new richness and fulfilment. But Lynda's instincts were awry on this one.

To her unfettered joy, Vicky was indeed pregnant.

When she suffered the heartbreak of learning that her longed-for baby had Down's Syndrome, and with Mike closing himself off, it was again Lynda to whom she turned:

VICKY — You will keep it to yourself, won't you, Lynda?

LYNDA — Of course. I won't breathe a word.

VICKY — I shouldn't have said. I promised Mike... but I just had to tell someone. And because you knew about the tests...

LYNDA — Yes... You must be devastated.

VICKY — I am. You always picture... when you think about having a baby, in your head it's always perfect. And I know I'm going to love it, but...

LYNDA You're... going to have it, then.

VICKY Oh yes. I couldn't do anything else. I couldn't.

LYNDA No. That's very brave of you, Vicky. And Mike... he feels the same way?

VICKY I don't think he does. But I can't do it without him.

LYNDA No.

VICKY I love him so much. But I have to have this baby. Oh, Lynda, what am I going to do...?

For Mike's part, it is Neil who is privy to his deepest fears.

MIKE I can't tell you, Neil... Waiting for the midwife to ring last week... It was one of the worst days of my life.

NEIL That's the hardest thing of all, isn't it? Not knowing.

MIKE Since then – every day's got worse. Like a big, black cloud's come down over both of us. And I can't see a way through.

NEIL How's Vicky taking it?

MIKE That's what's breaking my heart...

NEIL Oh?

MIKE She was so happy when she found out she was carrying. She thought she'd never have the chance to be a mother.

	This was like winning the lottery...
NEIL	Hmm.
MIKE	... until we found out she was one number short.
NEIL	Is that how she sees it?
MIKE	She wants to go ahead.
NEIL	What about you?
MIKE	I keep wondering whether it'd be better... if we didn't see things through.

As the pregnancy progressed, Mike overcame his initial fears. Lynda remained on hand when Vicky needed a friend and afterwards – and everyone in Ambridge was rewarded with the endless delight that a new baby brings.

DIPLOMATIC TIES

When David and Ruth moved into the farmhouse at Brookfield, the transition went surprisingly smoothly, except when it came to arrangements for Christmas. Jill was happy to cook but felt her new home, Glebe Cottage, was too small for a major family event and that Brookfield was a more suitable venue. Ruth was a reluctant host, fearing a spotlight would be left shining on her shortcomings in the kitchen. To David and Phil's frustration, neither would talk to the other about Christmas catering for fear of causing offence. Finally, David told Ruth about his mother's ambitions for cooking

Christmas dinner in her old kitchen at Brookfield.

DAVID	That's what she's been fantasising about, apparently, is you asking her to come and cook the meal here. For all of us.
RUTH	You're kidding.
DAVID	Nope.
RUTH	Why on earth didn't she say?
DAVID	The same reason you didn't feel you could ask her. You're both being too damn tactful.
RUTH	So if I did –
DAVID	She'd jump at it.
RUTH	Is she in now?
DAVID	Er, yeah, I think so.
RUTH	I'll phone her. Oh David, it's such a load off my mind.
DAVID	I know.
RUTH	It's been putting me right off my cattle passports.

SURROGATE PARENTS

Parenting is a challenge. And, just sometimes, outsiders can step in and make a better job of it than parents themselves. Take Ed Grundy, a drinker, a drug taker, occasional vagrant and low-grade criminal. Mother Clarrie was frustrated by his listlessness, while father Eddie became convinced he was a no-hoper.

The course of his life could have taken a nosedive without the intervention of Oliver Sterling, who saw something in the youngster that escaped most others in Ambridge. Ed impressed Oliver soon after he moved into Grange Farm by offering to help with maintenance. During the ensuing months, Oliver sought his advice about the herd and soon employed Ed to look after the cows.

Two years later, when Ed was charged with burglary, it was Oliver who offered to transport him to and from the Enhanced Thinking Skills Course which formed part of his punishment. In the car, Ed derided others on the course before being stopped short by some 'tough love' from Oliver:

OLIVER Just shut up and think for a moment, Ed.

ED Eh?

OLIVER You wonder why you've been put in a group with a bunch of what you call 'losers'? –

ED Too right.

OLIVER Can't you understand that to the outside world that seems exactly where you belong?

ED What? Me?

OLIVER Yes, you. To anyone who doesn't know you as a person you're just one of a bunch of losers.

ED No way.

OLIVER No-hopers. Set on the road to nowhere.

ED Not me. I –

OLIVER Now just listen. You've been extremely lucky to receive the punishment you have. You've been given an opportunity to take a serious look at yourself and to decide what kind of man you want to be.

ED But –

OLIVER You're not a child any more, Ed. It's up to you and you alone, to decide where you want to be in a year's time. In five years' time. And take the necessary

	steps to get you there. You've been given a chance so make sure you take it. You're a bright lad, Ed. There are a lot of people who are very fond of you.
ED	(WITH A LUMP IN HIS THROAT) I know.
OLIVER	And we all want to see you do well.
ED	Yeah, I know.
OLIVER	You'll get there.

Indeed, Oliver kept the faith and by 2009 was offering Ed the chance to be a tenant farmer at Grange Farm, loved and lost by the Grundys a decade previously.

To weigh the scales, it is Oliver's wife Caroline who proved to be William's saviour. She is William's godmother, emotional rock and financial support. This exchange occurred at a car auction in 2001 after Ed had written off William's vehicle in the accident that injured Emma.

CAROLINE	When I agreed to be your godmother, I wasn't really sure what it would entail. I've got other godchildren but they don't live nearby, I just send them a cheque on their birthdays and that's that.

WILLIAM	Right.
CAROLINE	But I've seen you grow up. I know what your life's been like, especially the last couple of years.
WILLIAM	Yeah, well.
CAROLINE	I'd like to make your insurance money up to £2,000.
WILLIAM	What?
CAROLINE	That's a gift. And to make sure you get something a bit decent, why don't I lend you another thousand on top, interest free. You can pay me back as and when you can.
WILLIAM	You can't do that.
CAROLINE	Why ever not?
WILLIAM	Well, because –
CAROLINE	Look, if you'd wanted to go to college that would have been an expense I'd be happy to help with. Well, you didn't but it seems to me a reliable car is a pretty good alternative.
WILLIAM	Caroline, I – I can't accept that sort of money.
CAROLINE	Yes you can.
WILLIAM	I can't.
CAROLINE	Well, you've got to because I'm not letting you buy one of these wrecks.

Could the odd-couple pairing with Jim Lloyd be the salvation of Jazzer? Jim rightly detected that Jazzer had never had a firm guiding hand, and indeed Jazzer's father, who used to call him 'Jackie', was a drinker who'd go anywhere for a free meal. To Jazzer's relief, he disappeared when Jazzer was seven, leaving him and brother Stu to be brought up by their mum. She's never earned enough to pay tax but does play bingo, though Jazzer feels that in family rows she always takes Stu's side. She's had various blokes over the years, having met some of them in the pub near the family home on the infamous Meadow Rise council estate, patriotically called 'The British Queen'. Jazzer remains in touch with his granny in Glasgow, Nanna, who once touchingly sent him a pair of Argyll socks for Burns Night.

Jazzer's reputation has hardly been pristine. After taking the horse pill Ketamine, he was hospitalised and suffered long-term brain damage. Perhaps his sometimes idiosyncratic behaviour stems from that distant incident. Certainly, as Jolene once remarked: 'Jazzer and common sense? You don't often see them keeping company.'

But surprisingly he quickly revealed he was prepared to learn from Jim's abundant library. Although he is sometimes challenged by Jazzer's domestic chaos, Jim was consequently ready to speak up on his behalf to son Alistair and daughter-in-law Shula as they tended to Daniel:

JIM	You see, this is the sort of parenting Jazzer's never had.
ALISTAIR	Probably because he's never spent his evenings doing history essays.
JIM	Cause and effect, Alistair. No one's ever given him any guidance. Or laid down any sort of rules, domestic or otherwise.
ALISTAIR	No, true.
JIM	He didn't start out with Daniel's advantages. And he's never had the opportunity for any sort of self-improvement.
SHULA	Hang on, Jim, are you saying you're going to give him that opportunity?
JIM	Where I can, yes.
ALISTAIR	The Noble Savage, eh, Dad?
JIM	Well, I don't intend to be quite that clinical about it, though I must say I'm finding it fascinating. But I'm not expecting miracles.
SHULA	Just as well. So you're going to let him stay?
JIM	Why not? I rather enjoy his company. And that's more than I can say for some people in this village.

IN THE MIDST OF LIFE

DEATH MUST INEVITABLY BE part of life as it unfolds in Ambridge. The village has suffered bereavements that leave in their wake feelings of numbness, emptiness, misery, horror, withering grief and sometimes painful guilt.

With the death of the elderly, there's a sense that the page has turned and a chapter is now closed. What remains is a batch of memories to be raked over, golden moments to be savoured and a collective amnesia that erases the foibles that once drove people to distraction.

Dan Archer had begun his agricultural life before the era of tractors and chemicals. He left it when farming had a very different impetus. When death claims people in their middle years, remorse comes to the fore for everything that might have been. There follow Christmas dinners with an achingly empty chair or holidays with an absentee mother or brother. Evenings that once would have been spent cosily with a partner are now endured alone.

Sudden loss brings about especially poignant regret; Nigel tumbling from a roof, Grace perishing in a fire and Polly dying in a car crash. Yet more grief-strickening still is the departure of the young, and John Archer's death when he had barely breached adulthood left a cavernous gap that is still notable.

Life goes on, however, even when the loss has been wretched and untimely. Those involved learn to master their sorrow and eventually raise their heads to the horizon once more. As long-time patriarch Phil Archer used to say, quoting an ancient Persian proverb: 'This, too, shall pass.'

A SUDDEN DEATH

A bewildering loss which sparked a tsunami of anguish, the demise of Nigel Pargetter sent shockwaves through the community like little that had gone before. He was young and fit, full of topsy-turvy wisdom and a vibrant asset to Ambridge. Even now his death remains a raw topic.

Former public schoolboy Nigel had always been a lively feature of Ambridge life, as Mr Snowy the ice cream man, a swimming pool salesman, environmentalist, doting father, loving husband and, latterly, a diligent businessman. Having inherited Lower Loxley in 1988, he cared passionately about it being a business and a pleasure.

Nigel plunged to his death from the slippery roof of Lower Loxley Hall on 2 January 2011 as he wrestled in the wind with an advertising banner. After his death Elizabeth, his wife of 16 years, was inundated with letters and calls, underscoring his popularity, and his funeral was packed.

For her and the children it was a personal tragedy that left a dark void. Before the funeral she told Usha: 'I just sit here with a hymnbook and a Bible. It is so unreal. How can I be planning Nigel's funeral, it can't be right. We should have had years and years together. I look at the words and they don't mean anything. My mind just goes blank.' To David, she said: 'I can't imagine anything after the funeral, just a great big black hole.'

Hoping to protect the children from high emotion, Elizabeth decided early on that they should not attend the service. Eventually, Jill persuaded her to change her mind after relating how, as a seven-year-old, she was kept from her own mother's funeral by a well-meaning aunt. It left the young Jill feeling that people you loved could disappear in a moment without saying goodbye, and bequeathed to her trust issues that extended into adulthood and were dispelled only when she met husband Phil.

Touched by this hitherto unknown part of her mother's life, Elizabeth changed her mind and the children flanked Elizabeth, dressed in purple, behind Nigel's wicker coffin which was pulled to church on a hay wagon drawn by his favourite Shire horse, Cranford Crystal. It was the same way Lettie Lawson-Hope, the wife of Ambridge's former squire, was delivered to her funeral in 1958.

Kenton held the congregation in laughter and tears as he recalled how Nigel had once helped Elizabeth escape from boarding school and later, how the pair were rival ice-cream sellers. Between them, he said, 'the romance never died'.

Later the South Borchester Coroner Richard Rushworth recorded a verdict of accidental death, having heard evidence from the dead man's brother-in-law, David Archer, who had been with him on the roof. There was nothing that David could have done to prevent the accident, the Coroner declared. Yet those words were scant comfort to widow Elizabeth, who gave a rocket to her brother for suggesting the roof-top activity during dubious weather conditions in the first place after guilt prompted him to confess it was his doing.

Freddie and Lily have also had a lot to cope with since the death of their father. As the first Christmas without him approached, the twins had a heart-to heart in which Freddie observed to Lily that it was up to them to 'make it seem as if we're OK' at Christmas 'just like we had to do on our birthday'. But Lily's grief boiled over when Freddie later took a tumble off Nigel's horse and broke his collarbone. Breaking down with her mother, Elizabeth, Lily accused Freddie of terrifying them and putting himself in danger. Elizabeth had no words with which to reply. She had already admitted to her sister Shula that what wrenched her heart was that, especially when around the horse, Topper, Freddie had such a look of Nigel about him.

A TRAGIC END

It's not the first time the entire village has grieved for a neighbour who has met an untimely end.

On 22 September 1955, Grace Archer, a young wife with a vibrant personality, perished from injuries sustained in a stable fire.

Phil broke the news to his father and sister in the kitchen at Brookfield: 'In my arms… on the way to hospital… she… she's dead.'

Just a few hours earlier, he and Grace, 26, had been drinking cocktails in the bar at Grey Gables with Carol Grey and John Tregorran, celebrating a successful day for Phil at the autumn sheep sales and, more importantly that Grace, who had previously wanted to delay having a family, had changed her mind.

Then, in a story that's been repeated many times over by Phil and others, Grace realised she'd lost an earring, went out to the car to look for it, and returned in a panic: the stables were on fire.

When Chris's horse, Midnight, having been led to safety, charged back into the flames, Grace, despite the fact that the roof was collapsing, ran in after her, followed by a frantic Phil. Inside, he found his wife pinned under a fallen beam.

PHIL	(COUGHING, BESIDE HIMSELF) Get it off her! Help me! Get it off! (STRAINS) Heave!
JOHN	(GRUNTS AND STRAINING) Can't budge it!
PHIL	Harder! Harder! (STRAINS) Heave, blast you! Pull your guts out!
REGGIE	(OFF, COUGHING) John! Phil!
JOHN	(YELLING) Here! Help! Tack room end! Hurry, Reggie, for God's sake.
REGGIE	(OFF) Keep yelling!
JOHN	(YELLING) Here... Here... (STRAINS) Buck up!
REGGIE	(COMING ON) I see you... strewth!
PHIL	(STRAINING) The straw under her's catching alight! Stamp on it! Don't let the fire touch her!
REGGIE	All right!
JOHN	(STRAINING) Get on this beam and heave, Reggie. Quick!
	(ALL GRUNT AND STRAIN)
REGGIE	(GRITTING) It's coming... Bit more... All together... Heave.
JOHN	Phil... Get her out while Reggie and I are holding it up.
PHIL	Grace... Grace...
JOHN	Buck up! Can't... (COUGHS) ... hold it much longer.
PHIL	All right. Got her!

JOHN	Get out! Quick!
	(<u>THUD, CLATTER, CRACKLE OF FLAME</u>)

Phil saved Grace from the flames and the assembled witnesses presumed she was simply out cold. But the injuries she sustained that night were internal and calamitous.

Conscious in the ambulance, she had the chance to tell Phil she loved him one last time. Reggie and John, meanwhile, trapped by advancing flames and showered with blazing hay, had to escape by smashing the tack room window. The rogue horse Midnight also survived the ordeal.

The whole family was devastated after Grace's untimely death in 1955, but Dan provided some heartfelt advice for hopeless and apparently helpless Christine on the circle of life:

> Me and Simon there… in the milking shed… we've got the same feelings as you and everybody else, but we've still had to carry on milking just the same as you've had to carry on feeding and watering those horses you've got here… and the same applies to breakfast and housework and ploughing and muckspreading and everything else, Chris. Life must go on, my love. It's heart-breaking and dreadful but it's not the end of the world. Life must go on for you, for Phil, for all of us. So let's all get busy and do something about it.

DEATH OF A COUNTRY GENTLEMAN

At the hub of the Archers dynasty for decades, Phil's death shook the family to its foundations and left an aching sore that would take months to heal. He died alone at home after wife Jill, sister-in-law Peggy and sister Christine had spent the day at an exhibition of hats through the ages.

Their trip had been punctuated with reminiscences.

JILL	Now that's what I call a hat.
CHRIS	(READS CARD) Sunday best. *Circa* 1959.
JILL	Imagine turning up at the village fete in that!
CHRIS	(LAUGHS) Oh yes.
PEGGY	That's where Phil first noticed you, isn't it Jill? What year was that? It must have been around that time.
CHRIS	Goodness, you're going back now, Peggy.
PEGGY	It was the year he filmed it all on his cine camera. The fete, I mean.
JILL	Nineteen fifty-seven.
CHRIS	He ran a cinema tent too! And wasn't that the year Humphrey Lyttleton opened the fete?

JILL	It was! I was working in Borchester. It was sheer luck I was there at all! It was scorching hot, do you remember?
PEGGY	That's right. I took all the children – he filmed them too – it was Lilian's birthday.
CHRIS	Was it?
PEGGY	I remember seeing the film. Lilian didn't want to go – she looked really sulky
CHRIS	So she'd have been...
PEGGY	Ten. Hard to imagine now!
JILL	This hat would have been just the thing on a day like that. Perfect for the sun.

They continued the amiable chatter as they arrived at Glebe Cottage, home to Phil and Jill since they passed Brookfield to David and Ruth a decade earlier, where haunting sounds of *The Dream of Gerontius* by Edward Elgar filled the air. (It was the orchestral opening to the start of part two which goes on to begin with the words 'I went to sleep'.)

Inevitably it was time to put the kettle on. Only when Jill went from the kitchen to offer Phil a cup of tea did she find his body, inert in a chair.

Afterwards, Jill struggled to come to terms with her loss. She broke down when Elizabeth discovered a card addressed to her mother in Phil's typically well-organised desk. It was for the forthcoming Valentine's Day and read: 'You bring me sunshine every day of my life.'

Toasting their father in the lambing shed the night before his funeral, Kenton called David 'a chip off the old block'. As David forlornly replied: 'They are big shoes to fill.'

The last photos taken of Phil were at Christmas, asleep with his party hat on, and these became dear to Jill.

Described in one tribute as 'one of nature's gentlemen', his death left St Stephen's without an organist, the National Farmers' Union short of an active supporter, the village cricket team bereft of an umpire – and granddaughter Pip asking: 'Why didn't granddad like sheep?' David gently explained that Phil was a pig man through and through.

In his eulogy, Alan, the vicar, said:

> Phil's vertical roots were fixed deep in Ambridge but so too was he woven horizontally into the fabric of village life. He was a man at the very heart of things; his family, the church, the wider community and the land. And not one you should regard just as a pillar of the community. I saw him rather as a village elder, keeping a quiet experienced eye on things, ready to give advice when asked but never imposing it, a man of impeccable judgement but never judgemental. A good friend and he lived a good life, a full life… He said to me once, though, the mysteries of the heavens were as nothing to the miracle of a calf being born and seeking out milk from its mother for the first time. Like the pole star, he was a fixed point in so many of our lives.

Symbolically born on St George's Day, Phil farmed like his father Dan had done before him and as his son David continued to do. The colourful patches of snowdrops and crocuses were blurred by teardrops as the congregation watched his burial.

TAKEN BEFORE THEIR TIME

Phil's end was timely but the same can't be said of his great-nephew John. Pat and Tony's firstborn died in a tractor accident on his brother Tom's 17th birthday, aged barely 22. Life had been complicated for John in the months before he died. He had split from his long-time girlfriend Hayley over his resumed affair with Sharon Richards, which remained an unpopular coupling with his parents.

But the night before his death, Sharon having left the village, John had taken Hayley out to dinner and proposed. Thoroughly confused, she'd turned him down. Next day, nagged by his father to mend a fence, John set off on the cabless Ferguson tractor that Tony had restored. But on a muddy turn, it slipped into a ditch, crushing him underneath it.

At teatime, with Tom complaining bitterly about his brother's lateness and selfishness ('This is seriously cutting into my party time!') and his mum and dad suspecting John was in a sulk, Tony decided he'd better see what John was up to. But out in the fields he made a horrific discovery:

TONY	Oh, John. (PAUSE) John! My boy! What have you done? (PAUSE. BENDS DOWN AND TOUCHES JOHN) You're cold. (BEAT) You're so cold. (TAKING OFF JACKET). Take my jacket, it's warm... (PAUSE) I'll stay and talk to you until someone comes. (STARTING TO CRY)

> Talk to you – what do I say? (PAUSE. TONY CRIES) Oh, John! John! (TONY CRIES)

The funeral was packed with young faces as his friends turned out in support. Touchingly unsure of how to behave and about what was appropriate in church, Hayley spoke about her former boyfriend:

> I'm proud to have known him. He was a great guy. Everybody makes mistakes, and we both made our share, God knows. I can say that, can't I? Yes. But that's not important now. What's important is to get him right in our minds. I wanted to find something to say about John. Roy said a lot of it for me in that poem he read. So I don't need to say what it feels like to miss him. Thanks, Roy. I know John liked this record and I listened to the words and I think they say a lot about how I feel about him now. So this is for you, John Daniel Archer. This is for you.

She then played 'Wonderwall' by Oasis.

And the poem that Roy had read, which had meant so much? It was only when someone asked the vicar, Janet Fisher, where it came from that it emerged that Roy had actually written it:

> I didn't know
> Until he went away
> How hard it is to show
> Or wear your feelings on your sleeve
> Hard even to think about him

Hard to grieve
He taught me this, I didn't know
That one day sitting in a room
I'd say: This is all mad,
Not how it's meant to go.
That door should swing
And in he'd come
Smiling and laughing
Like a likely lad.
But now I wait, and nothing's said.
The door stays shut,
And smiles and laughter dumb
I cannot think of anything to say
Perhaps we'll find fine words another day.
For now this has to do,
Words are all choked up
And will not flow.

At this point an emotional Roy took a pause before resuming:

We called each other 'mate',
Mostly the best,
We shared some laughs,
Some anger, never hate.
Feelings, they all felt part of it,
What human beings do.
He was a likely lad
That's all we need to know.
He's gone.

He was my friend.
It all seems wrong.
I thought we'd know
Each other till the end.

The suddenness of John's death shook the Ambridge community like a thunderclap. Tony – himself the firstborn Archer grandson for Dan and Doris – was racked with guilt having rowed with John. Mum Pat found it hard to recover, battling the despair that enveloped her for months afterwards. Surprisingly perhaps her most effective confidant was Mike Tucker, no stranger to depression himself.

It was not the last that was heard of John, however. A dozen years later Sharon's daughter Kylie made a reappearance in Ambridge where she spent her young years and put Pat in a spin when she mentioned a younger brother.

Counting back, Pat was the first to realise that John was probably the father of young Rich – although the boy knew Sharon's new partner Eamon as Dad. It was a nagging thought that simply would not go away, although she knew of the emotional hazards her probing could unleash. Finally, like many worried mums, she turned to Facebook, finding a picture of Rich on sister Kylie's page. He was the image of John, and Pat's suspicions were confirmed.

At first, there was unrelenting opposition to Pat and Tony meeting their grandson, with Tom, Helen and Sharon implacably ranked against them. Finally, each was talked around to the idea and a tenderly warm and fulfilling meeting took place at Bridge Farm, all the more poignant for being in the wake of Tony's heart attack.

Illegitimate heirs are nothing new in Ambridge. And, like so many others, Rich's existence could create serious issues in the years to come…

Solicitor Mark, Shula's first husband, died tragically when his car careered into a tree on a lane near Ambridge. He'd swerved to avoid Caroline, who was lying unconscious in the road after being thrown from her horse which had been scared by another, recklessly speeding driver. The irony was that both Caroline and Mark were on their way to Glebe Cottage where Shula and Nigel were waiting to stage a surprise hen night for Caroline, who was due to marry vet-cum-vicar Robin Stokes within days. Mark, 39, had agreed to be the girls' waiter for the night; Nigel was going to be 'Honest Nige' and take bets, as a racing evening was planned. None of it was to be. With her planned wedding postponed, Caroline lay unconscious for days, Robin at her side, talking to her and willing her to come round. ('The buds are opening on the hawthorn hedge. Like little green buttons. Oh, Caroline. Please wake up…')

Of course, Shula had also been at the hospital, not to see Caroline, but to identify her husband's body. She relayed her experience to her parents:

SHULA	All the way there – all the way down the corridor, I was thinking: I can't do this.

PHIL	Shula...
SHULA	But there wasn't a mark on him. You couldn't see the injury. It must have been the way they put his head.
JILL	Oh Shula...
SHULA	They all said he wouldn't have felt any pain. The sergeant said he'd have been dead the second the car hit the tree...

Like any parent, Jill's instinct was to want to make it all better. In private, she turned to Phil:

JILL	I just want to hold her and take all the pain away. Like when she was a little girl.
PHIL	I know.
JILL	I really don't think I can bear it. Seeing her hurting so much.
PHIL	We have to bear it, Jill. We mustn't let her down. She's going to need us.

Quite how much was yet to become apparent, because just before he died Shula and Mark had been for a second round of IVF treatment and throughout the trauma, local GP Richard Locke had continued giving Shula her hormone injections. She'd submitted to them numbly, but a week after Mark's death, Richard was able to confirm that she was pregnant.

SHULA	It's positive?

RICHARD Yes.

SHULA I really am pregnant?

RICHARD Yes, you are.

SHULA I'm going to have a baby?

RICHARD Yes.

SHULA (BEAT) Mark always said we could do it.

RICHARD So you hang on to it. For him.

The knowledge that after so many years of trying, and of disappointments, she was carrying Mark's child gave Shula, as she admitted, a reason to carry on. For her sister Elizabeth, though, things were difficult. Shula had been so distressed after Elizabeth's decision to abort Cameron Fraser's baby that the sisters had only recently been reconciled and now Elizabeth had to see her fiancé Nigel Pargetter seemingly drawn back to his first love as he supported his former girlfriend Shula in her grief. As Elizabeth cooked her father's breakfast on the morning of Mark's funeral, a perceptive Phil, knowing that as the baby of the family Elizabeth was used to everything revolving around her, found time to acknowledge her support.

PHIL You know we've really appreciated all the help you've given us this last couple of weeks.

ELIZABETH (POURING TEA) Oh, Dad. It was the least I could do.

PHIL I just wanted you to know it hadn't gone unnoticed. With all the attention on Shula.

ELIZABETH	As if I'd mind about that.
PHIL	I know you don't, love. But I'm sure it's meant a lot to her too.
ELIZABETH	I wish I could have done more... (TEARFUL) I wish – well, I suppose I wish I could bring Mark back for her.
PHIL	We all wish that, love.
ELIZABETH	Look at me. I haven't any right to cry.
PHIL	Of course you have.
ELIZABETH	I don't know how Shula's doing it. I couldn't.
PHIL	You don't know. Until it happens to you. (PAUSE)
ELIZABETH	Dad, what was Grace like?
PHIL	Oh, beautiful. Funny. Strong-minded – we used to have such rows. Still, we were both very young.
ELIZABETH	You must have been even younger than Shula.
PHIL	Yes. Yes, and I thought my life had ended. But it hadn't.
ELIZABETH	I suppose that's some sort of hope.
PHIL	There's always hope for the people left behind. Somewhere. Sometime. Eventually.

It's a conversation that has perhaps helped Elizabeth in the grim months that followed Nigel's death.

PUB GLOOM

When the drinkers of The Bull waved Sid and Jolene off on a holiday to New Zealand in 2010, no one had an inkling it would be the last time they saw him alive. Fallon was left in charge of the pub while the couple visited Sid and his first wife Polly's daughter Lucy.

It was in a tearful long-distance phone call from her mother that Fallon first heard the news of Sid's death:

> Something terrible has happened, love. It's Sid, he's dead. He went off for a jog before dinner. He were such a long time we had to go looking for him. We thought he might have got lost or summat. But there he was... There were all these people around. Someone sent for an ambulance. They tried, Fallon, they tried but it were no good. He was dead. What am I doing to do?

As shocked regulars gathered at the Bull for an impromptu wake, Kenton and Kathy went to tell Jamie the bad news. Jamie was Sid's son by former wife Kathy who, despite being divorced, inappropriately adopted widow's weeds. The popular publican died just days before his 66th birthday.

Peggy resisted the temptation to tell husband Jack about Sid's death. It was Jack who first showed faith in a wayward Sid when he turned up in Ambridge in 1963, giving him a job as a chauffeur and assistant despite his criminal record. Afterwards, Jack watched with some satisfaction as a fellow Brummie mended his ways, becoming a pillar of the community. Now Jack was ravaged by Alzheimer's and would not be able to process the news. Peggy left him in blissful ignorance.

This time the funeral would not take place in St Stephen's. Jolene and pregnant Lucy arranged for the service to be in New Zealand. Although they had split more than a decade previously, Kathy flew out with Jamie for the ceremony.

It was not the first time a cloud of misery had descended on the pub. When Polly died in 1982, it was a similar story, a normally happy atmosphere soured by tragedy.

Polly's death happened in the wake of a darts match triumph with the Viking trophy returning to The Bull from The Cat and the Fiddle. Neil, who was captain of the victorious team, taunted Eddie with a rhyme: 'Hey diddle diddle, the Cat and the Fiddle, The Bull is over the moon.'

A riotous night of celebration gave way to a mundane day in which Polly went shopping. When she crashed into the side of a milk tanker she was killed immediately although the tanker driver escaped without a scratch. Sid was dazed with grief.

SID	Polly's dead, Mrs P.
MRS P	I'm terribly sorry for you, Sid.
SID	Polly's dead – but I don't believe it.

Barmaid Clarrie could find few words of comfort.

CLARRIE	Isn't it dreadful?
MRS P	Yes, it is.
CLARRIE	Even Eddie's been flattened by it, and Joe went as white as milk when he told us – I thought he was going to have a stroke.

SID	Hello, Clarrie.
CLARRIE	Sid, oh Sid, I'm so sorry.
SID	Yeah.
CLARRIE	I knew I shouldn't have come – I feel terrible now.
SID	It's all right, Clarrie – I'm glad to see you.
CLARRIE	(SNUFFLING) I don't know what to say either. Aren't I a useless lump?
SID	Don't say anything.

Later that day Sid was left pondering the way life can change in an instant:

SID	What a difference a few hours can make, eh? Yesterday we were celebrating winning the Viking back – Tony was waltzing Poll up and down the bar, whole place full of laughter.
TOM	Easy now, Sid, easy.
SID	She's still around you know. Some warmth of her is still around – as if it was trapped in these walls where she lived.
PEGGY	I'm going to make us all a hot drink. And you must take those pills with yours, Sid, to make sure you get some sleep.

SID	I know it'll seep away – I know that – it'll go out under the doors and through the windows like warm air going to cold – and then…

Turning down numerous offers of a bed for the night, Sid stayed in the darkened pub lost in his thoughts about Polly.

A PATRIARCH'S DEPARTURE

Dan Archer died in typical farmer fashion, trying to right a fallen sheep he'd spotted in a field as he drove along with granddaughter Elizabeth. That he was 89 years old and had only just recovered from a bad chest didn't cross his dutiful mind, having seen an animal in trouble.

The pair had been talking about her forthcoming party, which he promised to attend. The catastrophe happened on his son Phil's birthday, who was left reflecting solemnly on a life intertwined. 'We were so close I never even thought about it. He was always there.'

The mournful atmosphere was shattered by Uncle Tom, though, when he came to tea soon after, to be served tea by Phil's sister Chris.

TOM	Two sugars for me, love.
CHRIS	It won't do your teeth any good.
TOM	These aren't my teeth.

A teenage Elizabeth was undoubtedly shocked by what had occurred, but her subsequent outburst as the family adopted what they felt was a suitably respectful stance by cancelling her party did her few favours.

ELIZABETH	And they took Granddad away in a sort of big plastic cello case.
CLARRIE	A what?
ELIZABETH	It was black PVC with a zip in it. Dad said it was like a bin liner.
CLARRIE	I suppose if that's what they use.
ELIZABETH	Well, Granddad doesn't care, does he?
CLARRIE	No, I suppose not.
ELIZABETH	And they've gone and cancelled my birthday party.
CLARRIE	What a shame. You were having it this weekend.
ELIZABETH	It was all arranged. I can't see the point of calling it off.
CLARRIE	As a mark of respect for old Mr Archer, I expect.
ELIZABETH	Granddad wouldn't want me to miss out on anything on his account.
CLARRIE	No, but even so...
ELIZABETH	And they kept me in last night. Wouldn't let me out for my birthday treat with Tim.
CLARRIE	Well, I expect there'll be another time.
ELIZABETH	There'd better be.

It was left to the vicar, Richard Adamson, in his eulogy to put some perspective on the death:

> When I first came to Ambridge, Dan came to visit me. Now I didn't really know anyone in the village and Dorothy and I had just moved all our tea chests into the middle of the living room, and we were standing there, feeling rather forlorn – and in he came. He had a cake Doris had baked for us in his hands, and we put the kettle on and we had a picnic tea on the floor. And after half an hour I felt as though I'd been living in Ambridge all my life because I saw it through his eyes. He knew and loved every square yard of this village, and nearly every person, and certainly every animal.

His death came six years after his eighty-year-old wife had passed away quietly in a chair, in the same way and at the same location as her son years later. Her body was found by granddaughter Shula after a tea party at Glebe Cottage, inherited by Doris after years spent in service with Squire Lawson Hope's wife Lettie. She and Dan had retired to Glebe Cottage in 1969 and, in another year, they would have celebrated their diamond wedding anniversary. For years she had been a steadfast feature of family life, the family's listening ear, and her children and grandchildren were left with a hole in their lives larger than any at first realised.

FARM PERIL

Farms are dangerous places. The death of Jethro Larkin, 63, who was killed by a falling branch in June 1987, is a fine illustration of the sombre point. He and David had been trimming overgrown trees by the farm track, an operation carried out regularly on tended land everywhere.

In the longer term, the tragic accident ushered in a new era at Brookfield with the arrival of agricultural student Ruth to replace him, and had an eventual happy outcome for David.

A guilt-stricken David took a long time to recover from Jethro's death, but the suddenness, shock and injustice of her widowed father's death was most felt by his daughter Clarrie. She was, by now, married to Eddie Grundy and was a busy farmer's wife and mother of two young boys. Back in the Grange Farm kitchen, Eddie and his dad, Joe, did their best to soothe her.

JOE	It wasn't so bad, when you think about it. He was out in the fields, doing his job. It's how he would have wanted it. That's how I'd like to go, when the time comes.
CLARRIE	I thought he'd just fallen over...
EDDIE	They said it was quick, he didn't feel a thing.
CLARRIE	I wish I'd got there sooner.

EDDIE	It wouldn't have done no good, Clarrie, love. You got there as soon as you could.
JOE	Out in the fields, with his boots on, doing a job of work. I can't think of a better way to go.
CLARRIE	They wouldn't even let me see him. I wanted to see him go, but they wouldn't let me.
EDDIE	Never mind, love, it can't be helped.
JOE	I dare say it was for the best. It's no good dwelling on it. I should try and put it out of your mind.
CLARRIE	I just haven't had the time, that's the trouble.
JOE	(PAUSE) Eh?
CLARRIE	I was going to do it this afternoon, but it's too late now.
EDDIE	Do what?
CLARRIE	They're still there, on the table.
EDDIE	What are?
CLARRIE	His trousers… (TEARS) I never even mended his trousers. (SOBS)

There was more pathos when Jethro's faithful border collie, Gyp, refused to touch his food, despite Joe and Eddie's coaxing.

JOE	Come on boy. You show me how you can eat your supper...
CLARRIE	Here, Eddie, why don't you try this?
EDDIE	Is that a cup of tea? I'm parched.
CLARRIE	It's not for you, it's for Gyp.
EDDIE	Eh?
CLARRIE	(BENDS) Here you are, Gyp. That's what you were waiting for, wasn't it? (GYP WHINES)
EDDIE	A cup of tea?
CLARRIE	He always used to share a cup of tea with Dad before he had his dinner. That's why he wouldn't eat.
EDDIE	Blimey.
JOE	He's drinking it.
EDDIE	You mean I'll have to make him a cup of tea, as well as his dinner?
CLARRIE	(SUDDEN, SOBS) Oh, Eddie!
JOE	Now look what you've done.
CLARRIE	What am I going to do without him?
EDDIE	(ARM ROUND) Come on, let's go back inside.
CLARRRIE	Oh, Eddie, it's not fair. Why wasn't it somebody else? Why did it have to happen to Dad?

Neither Joe nor Eddie had an answer to that.

AN ERA ENDS

In 1988 one of Ambridge's most charming eccentrics (catchphrase: me old pal, me old beauty) took his final laboured breath. Walter Gabriel died of pneumonia, in the care of son Nelson and long-term romantic interest Mrs P.

Jill was tortured by the thought that he might have survived if only he had gone into hospital. But Nelson felt the sands of time had run through for him. 'No, Dad's time had come. And I think he knew it all along.'

Initially subdued, the roguish Nelson soon recovered his verve, as revealed in a conversation with Kenton and Shula.

NELSON	Me? I'm fine. Bearing up under the weight of public sympathy.
KENTON	It must be a bit of a strain.
NELSON	I can't cross the road without being button-holed by one of Dad's old pals.
SHULA	He was a very popular man.
NELSON	Especially among the ladies, it would seem.
KENTON	Good old Uncle Walter.
SHULA	Are you being harassed by his old girlfriends?
NELSON	My dear girl, I never realised how many octogenarians there are in Borsetshire.

KENTON	How do you know they're octogenarians?
NELSON	Because they tell me. It's quite true. Ladies of a certain age seem to have a compulsion to tell me how horribly old they are.
SHULA	Poor Nelson.
NELSON	They grasp me by the hand, gaze tearfully into my eyes and tell me what a good man Dad was.
SHULA	Well, he was.
NELSON	Or a handsome man, or a generous man or whatever. I thank them for their sympathy. Whereupon they tighten their grip and announce, 'I'm eighty-eight, you know.'
SHULA	AAhh.
NELSON	Or 'I'm ninety-four, you know,' or 'I'm a hundred and six.'
KENTON	And what do you say?
NELSON	What can one say? 'You look it, my dear?' No, I smile back and coo, 'I hope you make it to eighty-nine', or 'ninety-five'.
SHULA	Or 'a hundred and seven'.

Despite the scoundrel image he chose to foster, Nelson proved to have a surprisingly big heart, accommodating Nigel's troublesome mother Julia with aplomb. Mysteriously, he closed the wine bar he ran for years in Borchester – a favourite watering hole for the Archer family – and disappeared to South America, where he died in 2001.

LOST IN THE FOG

Helen's boyfriend gamekeeper Greg lived by the gun and died by it too, ending his own life in a shepherd's hut on the estate for which he worked, in 1994.

A long descent into a dark night of depression had been charted, with Greg himself acknowledging his problems in a conversation with fellow gamekeeper George Barford.

> Years ago, not long after I passed my test, I was driving home late one night over the moors. I'd been to see a mate. And the higher I climbed, the foggier it got. I couldn't see a yard in front of the car. Creeping along in first gear I got completely disorientated. Couldn't figure out where I was. But what kept me going was; I knew where I was heading. Home. A nice warm bed. I could picture it. And I knew if I just kept on I'd get there. Well, that's how I feel now. I'm lost in that fog. But the difference is, George, I can't picture where I'm heading.

Yet to Helen he denied there were problems and refused to take tranquillisers or seek psychiatric help. Eventually she moved out of their home in a despair ushered in by his volatile moods and unreasonable behaviour.

At about the time he pulled the trigger, Helen left an answerphone message, hopeful of paving the way to a reconciliation. Understandably, she was dogged by guilt after Greg's death. Uncharacteristically, Brian – who had found the body – also suffered pangs of remorse. It was he who had piled the pressure onto Greg, ultimately forcing the younger man to quit his job.

George was a willing listener. He had also suffered depression so acute that he had attempted suicide twenty years previously with a cocktail of alcohol and pills. In common with Greg, he had a failed marriage behind him and an uncertain relationship with his children. In his case, however, barmaid Norah McAuley breeched the fortress of misery that George created and steered him back to a rewarding life.

DRINKING DILEMMA

When Peggy first met Jack Archer in the NAAFI canteen she – as a self-confessed 'wide-eyed, innocent townie' – was entranced with his tales of ploughing a straight furrow with Shire horses Blossom and Boxer in double harness. But, as the face of farming changed following the Second World War, Jack got stuck in a rut, failing to keep up with modern methods yet unable to focus on a new career.

Peggy complained to his parents Dan and Doris that he was being used as a 'rubbing rag' at Brookfield Farm. She favoured working in double harness with him herself at The Bull as a permanent remedy for his butterfly employment record. Little did she know how her carefully laid plans would beckon disaster. With alcohol readily at hand, Jack too often filled his glass when he filled those of customers and what started as a tipple turned into a monumental drink problem.

In 1967, Dan Archer and Uncle Tom were summoned to The Bull by a tight-lipped Peggy who'd found Jack unconscious in bed, with a poor colour and gasping for breath. Beside him lay an empty whisky bottle. He always took a good, strong nip first thing, she told them, 'to put him right'. His appetite had deserted him and his mental balance was delicate. 'I think he fought against the bottle – and lost,' she told them.

Jack's lack of self-worth was the root of his alcoholism. According to Peggy, it was a case of 'too much money to play with, not enough work to do – and loneliness.' He suffered the twin addiction of gambling, too. On more than one occasion Peggy threatened to break up the unhappy home by leaving him, with Jennifer, Lillian and Tony in tow.

Unsurprisingly, given the years of alcohol abuse, Jack's heart and liver were affected, leaving it difficult for him to function. It took five years for life to slowly ebb from Jack's wracked body. In the meantime, Peggy ran The Bull virtually singlehandedly – but initially found that his death made things even more difficult.

Her mother-in-law Doris was as ever on hand with advice, and Peggy's daughter Lilian was in a good place to sympathise too. She'd been widowed in 1970 when her first husband, Canadian Air Force pilot Lester Nicolson ('Nick') died unexpectedly. He was 23 and Lilian just 22 at the time.

DORIS	I don't think you ought to shut yourself away from your customers at The Bull, you know.
PEGGY	I know, Mum, but I don't think I could face them – not yet anyway.
DORIS	It just pushes you in on yourself and that's not right.
PEGGY	I can't argue with you, Mum – it's just a silly feeling that's all. And it's not as if I think they'll be unkind, just the opposite in fact.
LILIAN	Yes... but it's having to cope with so much sympathy that catches your throat, isn't it?

GRAVE PROBLEMS

The gloom surrounding tenant farmer Ken Pound's death in November 1983 – that of a disappointed man at the most miserable time of year – was compounded when the earth on his grave sank by a foot the week before Christmas. But it was more a case of 'peace on earth' when both Brian and Eddie, under pressure from their wives, converged on the churchyard with trailer-loads of topsoil to top it up. As the two had earlier fallen out over Grundy pheasant poaching, gamekeeper Tom Forrest ('When other kids was fishing for tiddlers with jam jars, Eddie was soaking raisins in whisky and using ball-bearings in his catapult!') was open-mouthed when they later repaired to The Bull and Brian bought drinks all round. Brian blamed the spirit of Christmas.

Neighbour Joe Grundy had been a good friend of Ken and his wife Mary and was a stalwart support to her in the days and months following Ken's death. One conversation took a surprising turn, though. It had started innocently enough with an idle remark about the perils of sunbathing:

JOE	The sun can do terrible things to you if you don't treat it with respect. Remember Silas Winter?
MARY	(HESITANT) Yes.
JOE	He went out in that blazing July hay meadow, didn't he, and took off his moleskin trousers. (LAUGH) Well, he were with Gertie Powell… least, I think it were her… but I do know that, having been burnt on a certain place, he couldn't sit down for a month after! (LAUGHS)
MARY	(SOBERLY) Some things are better left in the grave, Joe.

Quite so. Because it later emerged that it had been Mary, not Gertie, with Silas Winter that day, and that her daughter Marilyn, born the following year, was not her husband Ken's child…

JOE'S BRUSH WITH DEATH

'How much time has he got, do you reckon?' was all Joe Grundy heard of a phone call between his son Eddie and Ambridge's GP, Richard Locke, in 1995, but it was enough to convince Joe they'd been talking about him. (They were, in fact, talking about Neil Carter's Duroc boar – Eddie had wagered that the animal wasn't long for this world.) But as Joe's past life flashed before him, all he could think of were the *bad* deeds he'd committed, and he embarked on a tour of the village in an attempt to right a few wrongs. Villagers bemused by his behaviour included:

- Caroline – to whom he apologised for fleeing Grey Gables without paying for a bottle of champagne some years before (he still didn't offer to pay up, though)
- Jill – whom he asked if she really thought anyone who wasn't Church of England would get into Heaven (Joe being a Methodist)
- Marjorie Antrobus – whom he treated to dinner at Borchester's finest restaurant, Botticelli's
- His grandson Edward – to whom he gave his Uncle Enoch's pocket watch, though Clarrie later gave it back

- Ruth – to whom he promised hay at a fair price rather than the astronomical price Eddie had demanded
- Eddie and Clarrie – whom he treated to lunch at The Bull while quoting poetry at them

When Joe disappeared on Eddie's birthday, leaving him to do the milking, Eddie was furious, even more so when Joe returned explaining he'd been to Gloucester to see Eddie's elder brother Alf, hoping to 'mend some fences'. ('You'd have been better off mending the fence by the turkey shed,' snapped Eddie.) But Joe's birthday gift of a black tie – 'You'll get some use out of it' – did pique Eddie's concern, and over the next few weeks he allowed Joe to cut back on his farm duties and put his feet up, even going so far as to make a special trip to The Bull one evening to get his dad a bottle of brandy for his chest. Joe lapped up the treatment but, sure enough, his sins found him out when Richard told Eddie that, asked straight out, he'd disabused Joe of the notion that he was going to die weeks ago. Storming off, Eddie vowed he'd make Joe wish he was. In the meantime, however, in the course of his 'wiping the slate clean', Joe had almost managed to put a rocket under one of Ambridge's most totemic couples, Tom and Pru.

They may not have married until Pru was in her mid-30s and Tom in his late 40s, but Tom and Pru were inseparable thereafter until a series of strokes forced her to move into nursing care at The Laurels in the early 1990s. Tom joined her there a few years later, when he too became infirm, and the devoted pair died just six days apart. Before her marriage, though, Pru had obviously had her moments and Tom became suspicious when he visited her and found a vase of flowers in her room. Pru claimed they were from the staff, but, convinced that she had an admirer, Tom got Jill to drop him outside The Laurels on one of his non-visiting days, so that he could lie in wait for the Lothario. It turned out to be none other than Joe Grundy.

TOM — What the blazes are you doing here?

JOE — (THINKING ON HIS FEET) I'm visiting a friend. That's it! An old friend.

TOM — (DISBELIEVING) What old friend?

JOE — Erm… Jimmy. Jimmy Dawson.

TOM — Big Jimmy Dawson? The blacksmith? He en't in The Laurels. I'd have known about it.

JOE — He is an' all. You go and ask.

TOM — You're not fooling me. If I go in there you'll nip off sharpish! … Anyway, you en't come to visit Jimmy Dawson. Jimmy Dawson's six foot two with a tattoo of a snake on his arm.

JOE — So?

TOM — Why you brought him a bunch of carnations, then?

All was revealed when, a couple of days later, Joe finally confessed in The Bull. Tom had assumed widower Joe had taken a sudden fancy to 'my Pru' but it all went back many years earlier, to 1957, when Tom, then courting Pru, was on remand for shooting a poacher.

JOE	She was a handsome-looking woman in them days. Fresh as a spring morning.
TOM	Oh ar, yes, she was.
JOE	And I weren't a bad-looking feller, though I says so myself.
TOM	What's that got to do with anything? (A MOMENT'S SILENCE AS THE PENNY DROPS)
JOE	The flesh is weak, Tom.
TOM	I don't believe it! But... you was married at the time... and you had the two boys.
JOE	We did...
TOM	Are you saying you'd have left your Susan for my Pru?
JOE	If you'd been sent down for a few years who knows what might have happened? We're all slaves of passion, ain't we?
TOM	(DISGUSTED) You speak for yourself...
JOE	I ain't proud of what I've done.
TOM	Why drag it up now, then? After all these years?
JOE	The Book of Isaiah. 'Set thine house in order; for thou shalt die.'
TOM	You're a fine one to be quoting scripture!

JOE	It's my only solace. I want to stand before the Lord with a soul free from guilt.
TOM	I don't reckon it's the Lord you'll be standing afore!

To add insult to injury, Joe had, typically, let Tom pay for the beer.

A QUIET MOMENT

In Ambridge as elsewhere, the reaction to the death of Diana, Princess of Wales, in a car crash in Paris in 1997 was a mixture of disbelief, distress and grief for her young sons. At the time, the village was in the throes of rehearsals for *A Midsummer Night's Dream* – to be performed in the grounds of Lower Loxley. Jill was heavily involved in rehearsals but in the late evening she found herself craving a few moments' peace in the church, where Bert Fry found her:

BERT	Mrs Archer. Didn't expect to see you here.
JILL	I wanted some quiet after the rehearsal. (PAUSE) Difficult to concentrate on putting a play on at the moment.

BERT	I know. (PAUSE) But life has to go on... reckon the Princess would have wanted that, don't you?
JILL	Yes. (PAUSE) Can you give me a moment, Bert?
BERT	Of course.
	(JILL WALKS TO THE ALTAR. 3 OR 4 STEPS)
JILL	Lord, may the warmth and laughter and hope that I have known be handed down in trust to my children and children to come. May they live to know that whilst all things fade and die, love lives on.